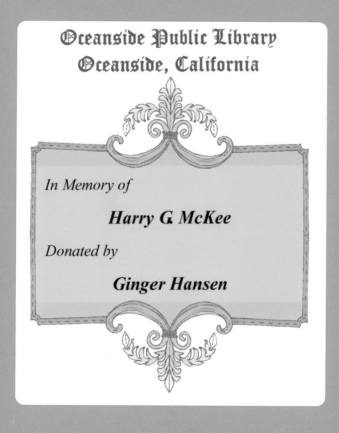

Dave's Dinners

Also by Dave Lieberman

Young and Hungry

Dave's Dinners

A Fresh Approach to Home-Cooked Meals

Dave Lieberman

Photography by George Whiteside

HYPERION

New York

Library of Congress Cataloging-in-Publication Data
ISBN: 1-4013-0129-0

Hyperion books are available for special promotions
and premiums. For details contact Michael Rentas,
Assistant Director, Inventory Operations, Hyperion,
77 West 66th Street, 12th floor, New York, New York
10023, or call 212-456-0133.

Book design by rlf design

FIRST EDITION

10 9 8 7 6 5 4 3 2 1

To my dear grandparents,

Bubby and Zaida,

who have brought

me much food

and much love

from the beginning.

Contents

Dave's Dinners

Introduction

As life gets busier, I find that dinner is really the meal I look forward to most. There are a couple of reasons for this. First, I've usually forgotten to eat during the day, so I'm pretty much starving. But second, it's the time of day when I can unwind and enjoy cooking. Even though I cook for a living, cooking still remains one of my main sources of enjoyment and relaxation. And it's still one of the best ways (if not the only way!) for me to get my friends together. But my friends are also busier than ever, so dinner is definitely the time when I have the best shot of gathering them. That's why I decided this cookbook should be about dinner. This is a collection of recipes I'm proud and happy to serve my friends and eat myself, night after night.

Dinner is also when my palate and my stomach are feeling most adventurous, so I can play around with all kinds of flavor combinations and ingredients. By focusing on dinner, I've been able to come up with a bunch of recipes that are creative and a little off the beaten path. This isn't to say that these recipes are extreme and avant-garde; they are simply good, tasty, streamlined recipes to make the kind of food I like to eat and others enjoy eating too. That's good enough for me. In each dish, I try to bring out the best from my fresh ingredients and make sure to include layers and contrasts of flavor, texture, and sometimes temperature to keep things interesting and exciting. All good food includes these elements, but there's no reason to be fussy about it.

Fortunately, dinner turned out to be the perfect topic for my second cookbook because it lets me talk about almost every cooking technique, from sautéing to shallow frying to braising. This is exciting for me because I get to introduce you to a few new things. However, you shouldn't need to update your kitchen drawers. All of my recipes rely on the most basic cooking tools: pots, pans, knives, cutting board, and the like. The most extravagant tools you will come across are a blender and a peeler. That's not to say there aren't a couple nifty gadgets worth having. An immersion blender or purée stick makes puréeing hot soups a whole lot quicker, easier, and cleaner. If your knife skills aren't impeccable, a plastic mandoline will let you make really fine, even cuts for everything from potatoes to fennel to radishes. Just be careful of your fingers.

Now I'll jump right into the recipes. Just remember to appreciate your time with good fresh ingredients, enjoy putting out delicious food, and bask in the pleasure of sharing food with people you care for.

Drinks and Finger Foods

Having dinner doesn't necessarily mean sitting down to a formal meal around the table. Sometimes dinner is better when eaten standing around with friends in the living room, drinks in hand. When the mood calls for the latter, I like to break out an arsenal of finger foods. And I take my finger foods seriously—no potato chips and peanuts here. As much thought and preparation, if not more, can go into finger foods as into a sit-down meal. It makes sense, actually—you have a much smaller piece of real estate and a much shorter time to make a good impression, so that finger food had better be darned good! You've got to fit all the elements of a good dish into one single bite. Luckily I've figured it out for you so all you have to do is follow the recipes.

A finger food dinner can wind up being more work if you don't get as much preparation done as possible in advance. Gather the elements and have them sitting either in the fridge or on the counter, ready to be assembled. This will make your life much easier and give you a chance to actually enjoy your get-together, maybe even have a couple of drinks yourself!

For years, I made my drinks with common mixers and liqueurs, but I'm growing out of that. Instead of depending on others to flavor my drinks, I figure I should take the same approach to drinks as I take to food: That is, make it my own. So I've started spending some serious time in the kitchen working on drinks. My favorite method to individualize my drinks is concocting my own infused syrups. They really couldn't be simpler: just sugar, water, and a flavorful ingredient or two. But the fresh infused flavors really make a difference. What I like best about them is that they make crisp, clean drinks. Most of the flavors I lean toward are herbal or citrus in quality, so I infuse thyme, rosemary, citrus rinds, lemongrass, and ginger. Spices are also fun to play around with, so I've included my recipe for Orange-Cardamom Syrup.

Drinks

All of these syrups are made the same way. You combine sugar, water, and the flavorings in a pot, and simmer the mixture until the syrup has reduced and infused with flavor. Then you cool them down. A couple of spoonfuls serves as the only mixer you need. **Here are my syrups:**

Rosemary Syrup

½ cup roughly chopped rosemary leaves
   and stems
½ cup sugar
2 cups water

Place all syrup ingredients in a saucepan and boil 30 minutes. Strain and allow to cool fully before use.

Ginger Syrup

¼ pound ginger, peeled and roughly chopped
½ cup sugar
2 cups water

Place all syrup ingredients in a saucepan and boil 30 minutes. Strain and allow to cool fully before use.

Orange-Cardamom Syrup

Rinds of 2 large or 3 small oranges
25 whole cardamom pods, cracked
½ cup sugar
2 cups water

Place all syrup ingredients in a saucepan and boil 30 minutes. Strain and allow to cool fully before use.

Lemongrass Syrup

5 large lemongrass stalks, cut into
   1-inch pieces
½ cup sugar
2 cups water

Place all syrup ingredients in a saucepan and boil 30 minutes. Strain and allow to cool fully before use.

Lemon-Thyme Syrup

Rinds of 3 lemons
1 large bunch thyme leaves and stems
½ cup sugar
2 cups water

Place all syrup ingredients in a saucepan and boil 30 minutes. Strain and allow to cool fully before use.

And here are my favorite drinks using these syrups:

Lemongrass Bellini

Pour 1 to 2 teaspoons of Lemongrass Syrup (page 7) into an empty champagne flute. Fill the glass with Prosecco.

Orange-Cardamom Bellini

Pour 1 to 2 teaspoons of Orange-Cardamom Syrup (page 7) into an empty champagne flute. Fill the glass with Prosecco.

Orange-Cardamom Bellini

Orange-Cardamom Apple Cider Rum Punch

1 ounce Orange-Cardamom Syrup (page 7)
2 ounces apple cider
2 ounces dark rum
2 orange pieces
Shaved ginger

Shake the syrup, cider, rum, and orange pieces on ice. Pour into a rocks glass. Garnish with a piece of shaved ginger.

Rosemary-Lemon Fizz

1 ounce Rosemary Syrup (page 7)
2 ounces vodka or gin
2 pieces lemon
Splash of soda
Fresh rosemary sprig

Shake the syrup, vodka or gin, and lemon pieces on ice. Pour into a rocks glass and hit with a splash of soda. Garnish with a fresh rosemary sprig.

Gin and Ginger

2 ounces Ginger Syrup (page 7)
2 ounces gin
Soda
Fresh rosemary sprig

Shake the syrup and gin on ice. Pour into a rocks glass and fill with soda. Garnish with a fresh rosemary sprig.

Rosemary-Lemon Fizz

Jamaican Fizz

2 ounces Ginger Syrup (page 7)
2 ounces dark rum
2 pieces fresh lime
Splash of soda
Shaved ginger

Shake the syrup, rum, and lime pieces on ice. Pour into a rocks glass and hit with a splash of soda. Garnish with a piece of shaved ginger.

Lemon-Thyme Martini

1 ounce Lemon-Thyme Syrup (page 7)
2 ounces vodka or gin
Lemons
Fresh thyme sprig

Shake the syrup and vodka or gin on ice. Strain into a martini glass and garnish with a twist of lemon and a thyme sprig.

Lemon-Thyme Martini

Ginger-Lemongrass Caipirinha

Ginger-Lemongrass Caipirinha

1 small lime, cut into eighths
1 ounce Ginger Syrup (page 7)
1 ounce Lemongrass Syrup (page 7)
2 ounces light rum, preferably cachaça
Splash of soda
Strip of ginger

Muddle the lime with the syrups and rum. Shake with ice, pour into a rocks glass, and hit with a splash of soda. Garnish with a strip of ginger.

Ginger-Cranberry Fizz

1 ounce Ginger Syrup (page 7)
2 ounces cranberry juice
2 ounces vodka or gin
2 pieces fresh lime
Splash of soda
Shaved ginger

Shake the syrup, cranberry juice, vodka or gin, and lime pieces on ice. Pour into a rocks glass and hit with a splash of soda. Garnish with a piece of shaved ginger.

Fried Sardines With Lemon-Relish Mayonnaise

My dad always told me that sardines were really good for me. He never mentioned that they could taste this good! My friends are sometimes reluctant to try these guys, but once they do, they always come back for more.

For the Lemon-Relish Mayonnaise

Juice of $\frac{1}{2}$ lemon

$\frac{1}{2}$ cup mayonnaise

$\frac{1}{3}$ cup sweet relish

About 10 grinds fresh black pepper

For the Sardines

2 ($3\frac{1}{2}$-ounce) cans sardines packed in olive oil

$\frac{1}{4}$ cup plus $\frac{1}{3}$ cup all-purpose flour

$\frac{1}{3}$ cup cornmeal

1 large egg

4 cups vegetable oil, for frying

> Oil-packed sardines are especially delicate, so handle them gingerly when you remove them and when you're battering them or else you'll break them apart.

Make the mayonnaise: Combine all the ingredients in a small mixing bowl and stir to combine fully. Transfer to a small dipping bowl.

Gently remove the sardines from the cans and lay out on a large plate. Dust them with $\frac{1}{4}$ cup of flour and toss to coat.

Whisk together the cornmeal and $\frac{1}{3}$ cup flour in a mixing bowl until combined.

Lightly beat the egg in a mixing bowl.

One by one, use a fork to pick up the sardines and dip them in the egg. Then dredge them in the cornmeal-flour mixture. Lay the prepared sardines on another plate ready for frying.

Heat the oil in a large saucepan or pot over medium-high heat for 5 minutes to about 350°F. Carefully slip the sardines one by one into the hot oil. Fry 3 minutes on each side, until golden brown. Remove the cooked sardines and transfer them to a plate lined with a double layer of paper towels to absorb the excess oil. Serve on a plate accompanied by the mayonnaise.

Makes about 12 sardines

17

Fried Mozz-Stuffed Olives

Stuffing olives with mozzarella is fun—and weirdly hypnotizing. Frying them up is pretty cool, too. Use smoked mozzarella if you can get it.

1 jar pitted green olives, about 8 to 10
    ounces when packed in brine
Olive oil
¼ pound mozzarella (preferably smoked)
2 tablespoons plus ⅓ cup all-purpose flour
2 eggs
½ cup yellow cornmeal
Freshly ground black pepper
4 cups vegetable oil, for frying

Drain the olives. Remove any filling from the centers, if necessary, and place the olives in a bowl. Drizzle lightly with olive oil and toss to coat.

Cut the mozzarella into pieces just small enough to fit into the hole of the olives. Stuff each of the olives with a piece of the cheese. Sprinkle 2 tablespoons of flour over the olives and toss to coat.

Heat the oil in a small pot over medium heat for about 5 minutes, to about 350°F.

Break the eggs into a shallow bowl and beat lightly.

Combine the cornmeal and ⅓ cup flour in a mixing bowl. Season lightly with pepper and toss to combine. Dip the floured olives in the beaten egg, letting any excess drip back into the bowl. Coat the olives all over with the cornmeal and flour mixture and place them on a tray or large plate.

Fry the olives in a couple of batches until golden brown, about 3 minutes, but not so long that the cheese oozes out from the center of the olives.

Drain the fried olives on paper towels to absorb any excess oil. Serve as soon as possible—the fresher the better!

Makes about 25 olives

International Puff Pastries

Even though these three puff pastry bites taste so different, I use
the same technique for putting all of them together. It's fun to watch
them get all puffy and golden brown in the oven.

Preheat the oven to 400°F.

Flour a clean, dry countertop or other flat working surface. Lay out a 10 × 9½-inch piece of packaged puff pastry, about ⅛ inch thick, onto the floured surface. Flour the top of the dough.

Roll out the puff pastry until it is half as thick (about ¹⁄₁₆ inch) and about 24 × 12 inches. Trim the edges to size if necessary.

Cut 3-inch strips crosswise and lengthwise making thirty-two 3 × 3-inch squares.

Make sure the squares are well floured, then stack them in a little pile.

Fill one pocket at a time: Fill a little dish with some room-temperature water. Imagine each square you work with is separated in half by a diagonal. Place a couple of teaspoons of filling in the top half. Dip a finger into the water and moisten the edges of the top half with water. Fold the bottom half to meet the edges of the top half. Use a fork to seal the edges.

Place the finished pockets on a nonstick baking sheet and bake about 10–12 minutes, until golden brown and puffy.

Makes 32 puffs

Spinach and Feta Filling

1 (10-ounce) package frozen spinach
6 to 7 ounces firm feta cheese
   (about 1½ cups), coarsely crumbled
2 garlic cloves, pressed
About 20 grinds fresh black pepper
Small dash nutmeg

Thaw frozen spinach either in the micro-wave according to package directions, or by leaving it out at room temperature.

Mix all the ingredients together in a bowl.

Samosa-Style Filling

1 large Idaho potato (about 1 pound)
Salt
2 tablespoons vegetable oil
1 small onion, finely chopped
½ pound ground chuck, 85% lean or higher
2 teaspoons curry powder
½ cup frozen baby peas
12 tablespoons plain yogurt
Juice of ¼ lemon
About 20 grinds fresh black pepper

Peel the potato and cut in half lengthwise, then in thirds crosswise to make 6 more or less even-size chunks. Place the potato chunks in a small pot with plenty of water to cover by at least a couple of inches. Add a few pinches of salt. Bring to a boil and cook until the potatoes are fork-tender, about 15 minutes. Drain.

Heat the vegetable oil in a large nonstick skillet over medium-high heat for a couple of minutes.

Sauté the onion until it starts to turn translucent. Add the ground chuck and curry powder and raise the heat to high. Work through the mixture with a wooden spoon or spatula to break up the meat as it cooks.

Cook until the beef is brown all over and most of the liquid given off by the beef has evaporated. A minute or two before turn-ing off, add the peas and heat until they start to turn bright green.

Remove from the heat immediately and transfer the mixture to a large mixing bowl.

Roughly mash the potatoes until crumbly, then add, along with the yogurt and lemon juice, to the mixing bowl.

Toss together all the ingredients until fully incorporated. Season to taste with salt and pepper.

Latin Black Bean

2 tablespoons vegetable oil
1 small onion, finely chopped
2 garlic cloves, pressed
1 teaspoon ground cumin
1 teaspoon dried oregano
½ teaspoon cayenne pepper
1 (14- to 15-ounce) can black beans, rinsed
4 ounces Cheddar cheese, grated
½ cup packed finely chopped fresh cilantro
   leaves

In a large skillet over medium-high heat, heat the oil. Sauté the onion and garlic until the onion is soft and translucent, about 5 to 7 minutes. Add the spices, stir to mix fully, then add the black beans. Cook until the beans are heated through, about 5 minutes, then remove from the heat and let the mixture cool fully. Add the cheese and cilantro and stir well.

Mini Fish Cakes With
Dijon-Shallot Caper Mayonnaise

I like my fish cakes light, moist, and tender. The trick to getting them
that way is not to use too many bread crumbs and not to shy
away from the mayo. Mayo is a beautiful thing!

For the Dijon-Shallot Caper Mayonnaise

¼ cup mayonnaise

1 tablespoon chopped fresh parsley

2 tablespoons nonpareil capers

1 tablespoon finely chopped shallots

1 teaspoon whole grain mustard

Juice of ½ lemon

About 15 grinds fresh black pepper

For the Fish Cakes

½ pound boneless scrod or cod fillets,
   minced

¼ cup plain bread crumbs

¼ cup chopped fresh parsley, plus more for
   garnish

¼ cup mayonnaise

About 15 grinds fresh black pepper

1 teaspoon ground coriander

3 tablespoons finely chopped shallots

1 teaspoon whole grain mustard

1 (6-ounce) can water-packed white meat
   tuna

1 egg, lightly whisked

3 tablespoons vegetable oil

Make the mayonnaise: Whisk the ingredients together in a small bowl until smooth.

Make the fish cakes: Mix the ingredients, except for the oil, together until the mixture holds together. Form the mixture into cakes about 1½ inches thick and 2 inches in diameter. Heat vegetable oil over medium-high heat for 4 minutes. Brown the cakes on both sides, about 3 minutes per side.

Top each cake with a dollop of the mayonnaise and garnish with chopped fresh parsley.

Makes about 20 fish cakes

23

Mini Flank Steak Tortillas
With Chipotle-Lime Sour Cream

These mini steak tortillas are a perfect hors d'oeuvre because they are a complete package stuffed with tons of flavor. And they look really nice, too.

For the Tortillas

2 tablespoons extra-virgin olive oil

3 garlic cloves, pressed

Juice of ½ lime

1 tablespoon Worcestershire sauce

1 tablespoon chili powder

1 tablespoon adobo sauce (from canned chipotles below)

½ teaspoon salt

15 grinds fresh black pepper

1½ pounds flank steak

For the Chipotle-Lime Sour Cream

1 cup sour cream

¾ teaspoon salt

1 canned chipotle, minced

Zest of ½ lime

1 large red pepper, stemmed, seeded, and thinly sliced

6 flour tortillas

½ bunch cilantro sprigs, tough stems removed

Combine the olive oil, garlic, lime juice, Worcestershire, chili powder, adobo, salt, and black pepper in a shallow baking dish and mix well. Add the steak and flip it several times to coat it well with the marinade. Cover and let marinate at room tempera-ture for 30 minutes or up to overnight in the refrigerator.

Make the sour cream by stirring together all the ingredients in a small bowl.

Heat a large skillet over high heat. Cook the flank steak about 4 to 5 minutes per side for medium rare. Transfer to a cutting board and allow to rest for 10 minutes. Return pan to the heat. Add the sliced red pepper to the hot pan and cook, stirring often, until softened, about 4 to 5 minutes. Remove from the heat and set aside.

Use a paper towel to rub the inside of the pan clean.

Toast the tortillas in the pan about 45 seconds to a minute on each side. Keep moist and pliable by sealing in a plastic bag.

To assemble the tortillas, slice the meat across the grain into thin slices. Cut the tortillas in half. Put 3 to 4 slices of meat and some red pepper slices into the center. Top with a dollop of sour cream and a couple of cilantro sprigs. Fold up and serve warm.

Makes about 12

Mini Moroccan Lamb Burgers
With Lemon Yogurt Sauce

I like making mini versions of things as finger food. No exception here.
I think ground lamb is one of the greatest bargains out there because the
meat is so flavorful and juicy. The point of the sauce is to be tangy and
refreshing to contrast with the rich flavors of the lamb burgers.

For the Mini Burgers

1$\frac{1}{2}$ pounds ground lamb
$\frac{1}{2}$ teaspoon ground cumin
$\frac{1}{2}$ teaspoon ground cinnamon
$\frac{1}{2}$ teaspoon ground coriander
1 teaspoon salt
About 20 grinds fresh black pepper
2 garlic cloves, pressed

For the Lemon Yogurt Sauce

7 ounces plain yogurt, preferably full fat
Juice and zest of $\frac{1}{2}$ lemon, plus more lemon
　　zest for garnish
Salt

1 loaf fresh brioche bread

Preheat the oven to 500°F.

Make the burgers: Combine all the ingredients in a mixing bowl and work together until they are fully incorporated.

Roll a tablespoon of the mixture into a 3-inch ball and then flatten into a round burger about $\frac{1}{2}$ inch thick.

Place the mini burgers on a nonstick baking sheet and bake about 7 minutes, until evenly and well browned.

Make the sauce: Stir together the yogurt, lemon juice, and zest in a small bowl. Season to taste with a couple of pinches of salt

Cut the brioche into $\frac{1}{2}$-inch slices, then use a small glass to cut as many circles as possible, about 3 inches in diameter, from each slice. Place the bread circles on a baking sheet. When the burgers come out of the oven, slip the bread in for just a couple of minutes to toast lightly. Watch the bread carefully, or else it will get too dark very quickly.

Place the mini burgers on top of the cut brioche. Top with a dollop of the lemon yogurt and garnish with a good pinch of lemon zest.

Makes about 30 burgers

Mini Potato Latkes
With Apple-Pear Chutney

My dad used to make fresh potato latkes for me and the family at least a couple of times a year and we would eat them hot out of the pan with tons of applesauce. Here's my grown-up version.

For the Chutney

2 tablespoons vegetable oil

1 pound Golden Delicious apples, peeled, cored, and cut into ½-inch cubes

1 pound Bosc or Comice pears, peeled, cored, and cut into ½-inch cubes

1 medium red onion, finely diced

1 (1-inch) piece ginger, peeled and grated

⅓ cup sugar

¼ cup white vinegar

For the Latkes

1 pound Idaho or russet potatoes

2 eggs

2 tablespoons chopped fresh parsley

Few pinches salt

⅓ cup vegetable oil

Sour cream

Make the chutney: In a saucepan, heat the oil over medium-high heat. Add the apples, pears, onion, and ginger and sauté until the mixture starts to soften, about 10 minutes, stirring regularly. Add the sugar and vinegar and stir to incorporate. Lower the heat to medium-low and simmer for 50 minutes, until the mixture is soft and thick but the apples and pears still hold their shape slightly. Set aside to cool. Cool fully before serving.

When the chutney is cool, make the latkes: Preheat the oven to 250°F.

Peel and roughly grate the potatoes and put into a large bowl of cold water. In a large mixing bowl, whisk the eggs lightly, then whisk in the parsley. Strain the potatoes from the water and squeeze out as much water as possible. Add the strained potato gratings to the egg mixture, season to taste with salt, and mix thoroughly.

Heat the vegetable oil in a large skillet over medium-high heat for 4 minutes. Use about 2 tablespoons of potato mixture for each latke. First drop the mixture in the oil, then use a fork to flatten out the pancake.

Cook about 5 minutes per side, until golden brown. When finished, transfer to a plate lined with a double layer of paper towels to absorb the excess oil, then transfer to a baking sheet to keep warm in the oven.

When ready to serve, top each pancake with a dollop of sour cream and a dollop of chutney.

Makes about 15 latkes

Pan-Grilled Spicy Coconut Shrimp

Since shrimp are on the expensive side, this is one of the more indulgent finger foods that I'll put out. When it tastes this good it's worth it! My favorite part is the sweet and savory combination. And the Thai flair from the basil, lime, and coconut is really nice.

2 small fresh jalapeños or red chili peppers, sliced
3 garlic cloves, thinly sliced
1 ($1/2$-inch) piece fresh ginger, peeled and grated
2 tablespoons dark brown sugar
2 tablespoons soy sauce
Zest of $1/2$ lime
$1/4$ cup coconut milk
Small handful basil leaves, torn
2 tablespoons vegetable oil
$1/2$ teaspoon salt
15 grinds fresh black pepper
1 pound peeled, deveined shrimp
Wooden skewers

In a mixing bowl, combine the jalapeños, garlic, ginger, brown sugar, soy sauce, lime zest, coconut milk, basil, vegetable oil, salt, and pepper. Add the shrimp and marinate at room temperature for at least 30 minutes and up to 4 hours refrigerated.

String a couple of shrimp onto wooden skewers that have been soaked in water for at least $1/2$ hour.

Heat a grill pan over high heat until smoking hot, about 5 minutes. Remove the shrimp from the marinade and place in an even layer in the pan, reserving the marinade.

Cook the shrimp until well browned on each side, turning once, about 3 to 4 minutes total. Transfer the cooked shrimp to a serving plate.

Turn the heat off. Add the reserved marinade to the pan, let thicken for a minute or two, then pour off the reduced marinade into a small serving bowl and serve alongside the grilled shrimp.

Makes about 15 skewers

Roasted Red Peppers and Ricotta Crostini

Ricotta is one of my favorite ingredients of all time. You've got to go with the full-fat kind, though, to truly experience the joy of it. The sweetness of the peppers, the freshness of the sprouts, and the tang of the vinegar play off the rich ricotta.

4 red peppers

1 fresh baguette, cut on an angle into
  ¼-inch slices

½ cup balsamic vinegar

1½ cups ricotta cheese

40 grinds fresh black pepper

1 container broccoli, radish, or pea sprouts,
  stems trimmed

Roast the red peppers: Char the peppers over a gas burner or under the broiler until well blackened and softened. Place in a sealed plastic bag or in a glass bowl covered with plastic wrap. Let sit 15 minutes. Peel and seed the peppers (the skins should pull away easily). Slice the flesh into strands about ⅛ inch thick.

Preheat the oven to 350°F.

To make crostini, lay bread slices on a baking sheet and bake about 7 minutes, until they take on a little color.

Place the vinegar in a skillet over high heat. Reduce by half and set aside to cool fully.

Mix the ricotta together with the black pepper in a bowl.

Top each crostini with a tablespoon-size dollop of ricotta, then heap several strands of red pepper on top and garnish with a pinch of sprouts.

Finish by drizzling the reduced vinegar over the top.

Makes about 25 crostini.

Ricotta-Stuffed Bacon-Wrapped Dates

These are the new pigs in a blanket, and way better. They're a classic tapas, but they never get old. I spruced them up just a bit with a touch of ricotta cheese.

1 pound bacon, sliced
⅓ cup ricotta cheese
40 pitted dates (about ¾ pound)

Preheat oven to 500°F.

Cut the bacon slices in half to make twice as many slices.

Place the ricotta in the bottom corner of a strong plastic bag. Use a scissors to cut a small hole in the tip of the corner. Use the bag as a piping bag to fill the dates with the cheese.

Wrap the ricotta-stuffed dates with a slice of bacon and secure with a toothpick through the belly of the date.

Arrange all the prepared dates on a baking sheet, allowing at least a little space between each one for good browning.

Roast about 10 minutes until bacon is dark brown and crispy and ricotta starts to brown where it is exposed. Serve hot.

Makes 40 bacon-wrapped dates

Roasted Tomato and Goat Cheese Tart

Here's another way to take advantage of that supermarket wonder,
puff pastry. This looks so beautiful when it comes out of the oven, it's almost
a crime to cut it up. But it would be a greater crime not to eat it.

8 plum tomatoes, halved lengthwise
Extra-virgin olive oil
Salt and freshly ground black pepper
2 garlic cloves, finely chopped
About 20 fresh thyme sprigs
1 sheet frozen puff pastry, thawed
2 ounces fresh goat cheese

Preheat the oven to 400°F.

Put the tomatoes on a baking sheet and drizzle them generously with olive oil. Toss to coat evenly, then place them cut-side up. Season the tomatoes with salt and pepper to taste and sprinkle the chopped garlic evenly over each tomato. Lay about 12 to 15 thyme sprigs over the tomatoes. Roast the tomatoes in the oven until soft but still holding their shape, about 25 minutes. Remove from the oven and allow to cool slightly. Then pinch off the skins, being careful not to damage the shape of the tomatoes.

Unfold the puff pastry onto another baking sheet. Brush the surface of the pastry well with olive oil. Lay the tomatoes, cut-side up, evenly over the pastry, leaving a 1-inch border around the edge. Fold the pastry edges up, creating a $\frac{1}{2}$-inch border. Press the edges to seal and brush with olive oil. Season the tomatoes with a little more salt and pepper and bake until the crust begins to puff and brown, about 20 minutes. Carefully remove the tart from the oven and crumble the goat cheese evenly over it. Return the tart to the oven and bake until the cheese begins to brown and the crust is golden, about 10 minutes longer.

Allow the tart to cool slightly before cutting and serving.

Serves 20

Smoked Salmon Nigiri
With Avocado-Wasabi Cream

I love sushi as much as much as the next guy, but the rolls can
be tricky to make and I like this presentation better anyway.
This combination is my go-to favorite. You could probably snag enough
wasabi paste for this from a friendly sushi bar, but if you can't, just
buy a little can of powdered wasabi and make it yourself.

For the Rice

1 cup sushi rice
1¼ cups water
2 tablespoons rice wine vinegar
2 teaspoons sugar
1 teaspoon salt

For the Avocado-Wasabi Cream

1 ripe Hass avocado, pitted and flesh
   scooped out
1 tablespoon wasabi paste
Juice of 1 small lemon

For the Sauce

⅓ cup soy sauce
4 teaspoons rice wine vinegar
½ teaspoon dark sesame oil
Zest of ½ lemon used for the
   Avocado-Wasabi cream

4 ounces smoked salmon, thinly sliced
1 small bunch scallions, trimmed and
   thinly sliced

Combine the ingredients for the rice in a
large saucepan. Bring to a simmer and
cook for 25 minutes. Remove the lid and
stir gently a couple of times. Allow to cool
fully.

Place the avocado and wasabi paste in a
blender and blend till smooth. Transfer to
a small bowl and mix in the lemon juice.

Mix all the sauce ingredients together in
a small bowl.

When the rice is cool, wet your hands and
form the rice into small oblong heaps.

Use a small spoon to top each rice heap
with a slice of salmon and a dollop of
wasabi cream. Arrange the pieces on a
serving platter. Top with sliced scallions,
serve with the sauce, and garnish with the
remaining lemon zest.

Makes about 15 nigiri

Three Colorful Dips

More than their delicious flavor, I love the color of these dips, especially when you serve all of them together! Serve with whatever kinds of crispy crackers you can get your hands on. Cut fresh veggies also work nicely.

Cauliflower and Almond Dip

1 head cauliflower, stemmed and separated
   into florets
1 bay leaf
4 ounces cream cheese
1 cup whole unpeeled almonds
1 small garlic clove, pressed
2 teaspoons salt

Bring a large pot of heavily salted water to a boil over high heat. Add the cauliflower and bay leaf and cook until the cauliflower is falling apart, about 20 minutes. Remove the bay leaf, reserve ¼ cup of the cooking water, and drain.

Transfer the cauliflower to a blender jar with the reserved cooking water and the remaining ingredients. Turn the blender on low and begin blending, then increase the speed to high to make a smooth purée.

Makes about 2 cups

Beet and Goat Cheese Dip

4 medium beets, trimmed
4 ounces soft, creamy goat cheese
Juice of ½ lemon
1 large shallot, minced
2 teaspoons chopped fresh thyme leaves
Salt

Submerge the beets in a large pot of cold water and bring to a boil over high heat. Cook the beets until tender and a knife slides easily into them, about 40 minutes. Drain the beets and cool completely. Using a paper towel, peel the beets, then grate on the fine holes of a box grater into a bowl. Stir in the remaining ingredients until well mixed and season to taste with salt.

Makes about 1½ cups

Pea and Leek Dip

2 leeks, woodiest part of the green leaves
    removed
2 tablespoons extra-virgin olive oil
1 pound frozen peas
$\frac{1}{2}$ cup sour cream
$1\frac{1}{2}$ teaspoons salt
$\frac{1}{2}$ cup fresh flat-leaf parsley leaves
Juice of $\frac{1}{2}$ lemon
2 tablespoons sliced scallions

Halve the leeks, cut into $\frac{1}{4}$-inch-thick slices, and wash well; drain. Heat the olive oil in a skillet over medium heat. Add the leeks and cook until softened but not brown, about 5 minutes. Add the peas and continue cooking until the peas are thawed and bright green, about 3 minutes.

Transfer the peas and leeks to a blender along with the sour cream. Blend on low until smooth, then add the remaining ingredients and blend until smooth.

Makes about 2 cups

Three Mini Open-Faced Sandwiches

Here in New York City, the deli sandwich is a big deal; everyone loves it. I love it, too. So much, in fact, that it inspired a little tasting plate of open-faced deli-style sandwiches, with a few of my own personal touches, of course.

Tarragon-Coriander Egg Salad With Gherkins on Pumpernickel

10 hard-boiled eggs

6 tablespoons mayonnaise

1 small bunch fresh tarragon, leaves finely chopped

2 teaspoons ground coriander

½ lemon, juiced and zested

½ teaspoon salt

About 15 grinds fresh black pepper

1 large shallot, minced

1 teaspoon grainy Dijon mustard

1 package party pumpernickel

10 gherkins, thinly sliced from top to bottom

Preheat oven to 350°F.

In a bowl, break up the hard-boiled eggs with a fork until they are coarsely crumbled. Add the mayonnaise, tarragon, coriander, lemon juice, salt, pepper, shallot, and mustard. Stir together well.

Use the rim of a small glass to cut the crusts away from the slices of bread in a circular pattern or simply cut away with a knife into a square. Place the bread on a baking sheet and bake until lightly toasted, about 5 minutes. Place a spoonful of egg salad in the middle of a toasted bread slice and top with sliced gherkins and some lemon zest.

Makes about 25

Warm Chicken Salad Bites
With Cranberry Compote on Rye

8 ounces fresh or frozen whole cranberries

Juice and zest of 1 navel orange

½ cup sugar

½ cup water

1 teaspoon fennel seeds

1 small, dense loaf rye bread

1 small rotisserie chicken, about 3 pounds

½ cup mayonnaise

Salt and freshly ground black pepper

Preheat the oven to 350°F.

In a saucepan over medium heat, combine the cranberries, orange juice and zest, sugar, water, and fennel seeds. Bring to a boil, then reduce the heat to low and simmer about 10 minutes until the cranberries break down and the mixture thickens. Remove from the heat and allow to cool.

Cut the bread into ¼-inch slices and place on a baking sheet. Bake in the oven until lightly toasted, about 7 minutes.

Remove the meat from the chicken and shred. Fold the mayonnaise into the chicken and season with salt and pepper to taste.

To assemble, place about 2 tablespoons of the chicken salad on each pumpernickel toast and top with a small spoonful of cranberry compote.

Makes about 25

Roast Beef and Watercress
With Horseradish Cream on Sourdough

1 dense loaf fresh sourdough bread

¾ cup sour cream

¼ cup bottled white horseradish, excess liquid strained

About 15 grinds black pepper

½ teaspoon salt

½ pound thinly sliced good deli roast beef

1 small bunch watercress, rinsed and leaves picked from stems

Preheat oven to 350°F.

Slice the bread in half and then into ¼-inch slices. Lay the slices on a baking sheet and toast lightly in the oven, about 7 minutes.

Mix together the sour cream, horseradish, pepper, and salt in a small bowl.

Place a dollop of horseradish cream on a piece of toasted bread, top with a slice of roast beef, and finish with a couple of watercress leaves.

Makes about 25

45

Veggie and Pork Potstickers With Citrus-Soy Dipping Sauce

Potstickers have long been a favorite of mine on the take-out menu, and in thinking about a finger-food menu I realized they would be the perfect addition. So I figured out how to make them (quite simple, it turns out) and tweaked the flavors until I was happy. You'll probably find the wonton wrappers in the produce or dairy section. Although I'm a big sucker for the pork dumplings, the veggie ones are darn good, too. It's nice to serve both just in case my vegetarian friends stop by.

For the Veggie Filling

1 tablespoon vegetable oil

1 leek, cleaned and thinly sliced

About 3 cups finely shredded napa cabbage from 1 small head

1 garlic clove, pressed

1 tablespoon rice or white wine vinegar

1 medium carrot, grated on the finest holes of a box grater

1 (1-inch) piece fresh ginger, peeled and grated

2 teaspoons soy sauce

Heat the oil in a large nonstick skillet over medium heat. Add the leek and cook until it begins to soften, about 4 minutes. Add the cabbage, garlic, and vinegar and cook, stirring, until the cabbage is soft, about 4 minutes more. Remove from the heat and stir in the carrot, ginger, and soy sauce. Allow the filling to cool.

For the Pork Potstickers

1 pound ground pork

1 egg

2 tablespoons finely sliced scallion

1 garlic clove, pressed

½ teaspoon sesame oil

1 tablespoon light soy sauce

1 tablespoon rice wine vinegar

1 (½-inch) piece fresh ginger, peeled and finely grated

Combine all the ingredients in a mixing bowl and work together until fully incorporated. Keep refrigerated until ready to use.

continued

{ The best way to clean a leek: Whittle away the tough green leaves, leaving the tender whites. Cut the leek in half lengthwise, rinse under cold water from top to bottom so the grit in between the leaves runs out the bottom.

DAVE'S DINNERS

Veggie and Pork Potstickers
With Citrus-Soy Dipping Sauce *(continued)*

To make the Potstickers

1 pack square wonton wrappers
½ cup water
1 tablespoon vegetable oil
Citrus Dipping Sauce (recipe follows)

Lay a wonton wrapper on the work surface and put a heaping teaspoon of filling in the center. Dip your finger in a little water and wet the edges of the wonton wrapper. Pinch the edges together to form four right angles.

To cook the potstickers, heat the oil in the skillet over medium-high heat. Place all of the potstickers upright into the pan and

cook, without disturbing them, until browned on the bottom, just a couple of minutes. Add the water to the pan and immediately cover. Allow the potstickers to steam for about 3 minutes, then remove the skillet lid. Continue cooking until the water has nearly evaporated.

Transfer the dumplings to a platter and serve with the dipping sauce.

Makes about 30

Citrus-Soy Dipping Sauce

¼ cup light soy sauce
1 (½-inch) piece fresh ginger, peeled, and
  finely grated
1 teaspoon dark brown sugar
½ teaspoon toasted sesame oil
Zest and juice of 1 lemon

Stir all the ingredients together in a small bowl until the sugar is dissolved.

Makes about ⅓ cup

Winey Figs, Prosciutto, and Ricotta Crostini

This is a combination of some of my favorite Italian ingredients. I love the creaminess of the ricotta with the sweet acidity of the wine-poached figs. That's why I always go with full-fat ricotta.

15 to 20 dried figs, preferably Calimyrna
2 cups full-bodied red wine
1 small baguette
1½ to 2 cups ricotta cheese
¼ pound prosciutto

Place the figs and wine in a small saucepan, bring to a simmer over medium-low heat, and simmer about ½ hour, until the figs have absorbed most of the wine and they are tender and fat. Some reduced wine should remain for the sauce.

Preheat the oven to 350°F.

Slice the baguette on an angle into ½-inch slices. Lay the bread slices on a baking sheet and toast lightly in the oven, about 5 minutes.

Spread a tablespoon of ricotta on each crostini, then lay a small piece of prosciutto on top of the cheese. Place a half or whole fig (depending on the size) on top of the meat and finish by drizzling the remaining reduced wine on top of the figs.

Makes about 25

The softer the figs, the better. They will also take much less time to soak up the wine and get juicy. Calimyrna figs are usually the most consistent in the tender and fleshy department.

Dandelion Greens with Beet Dressing and
Shaved Goat Gouda, page 66

Salads

It's pretty hard to make a bad salad. As long as you start with fresh greens and make a simple vinaigrette, you're pretty much in good shape. The most important part is freshness. That's why it's key to shop for salads seasonally. Many greens, such as the basic kinds of lettuces, are available all year-round. But some are harder to find at certain times of the year, such as dandelion greens or baby lettuces. Don't sweat it. It's not worth tracking down greens that aren't in season—you probably won't get good stuff in the end anyhow. You're better off substituting a green that's in full swing. If you can't get arugula, go for delicate spinach. If you can't find red leaf lettuce, try Boston. Of course, I choose the ingredients for my salad carefully for things like taste, color, and texture, but if you can't find one of the ingredients I've chosen, be flexible and mix in something else you think you'd like. I've also included some salads with the winter season in mind. These salads depend on traditionally winter greens such as fennel. I also bulk up my winter salads with things like squash, apples, and nuts.

Edamame and Scallion Slaw
With Orange-Lime Dressing

Edamame is the Japanese word for soybean and they're incredible! They're rich yet light, firm yet chewy, one of the few vegetables I know so full of contradictions. I first tried these in Hawaii at a Japanese restaurant. They were served in the pod and seasoned with tons of salt. I fell in love. Here, I just use the beans. You can buy them just like that, usually in the frozen or refrigerated section of the market.

For the Dressing

¼ cup olive oil
1 tablespoon whole grain Dijon mustard
Juice of 2 large navel oranges
Juice of 1 lime
2 tablespoons red wine vinegar
Salt and freshly ground black pepper

For the Salad

2 (1-pound) packages prepared slaw mix
1 pound edamame, shelled, boiled in salted
    water for 3 to 5 minutes, and drained
1 bunch scallions (about 6), thinly sliced

Combine the dressing ingredients in a bowl and whisk to combine. Combine the slaw, edamame, and scallions in a serving bowl. Toss with the dressing and serve.

If not serving immediately, cover the salad with a moist paper towel or clean kitchen towel and refrigerate until ready to serve. Dress the salad just before serving.

Boston Lettuce and Avocado Salad With Lime Dressing

I love the tender sweetness of Boston lettuce, but I'm always
eating it with creamy dressing. So for a change I came up with this
clean, tangy dressing with a little bit of a Latin twist.

For the Salad

2 medium heads Boston lettuce, any wilted
leaves discarded
1 Hass avocado, pitted
1 large bunch scallions, thinly sliced
Leaves from 1 bunch flat cilantro, finely
chopped

For the Dressing

Juice of 2 limes
$\frac{1}{3}$ cup extra-virgin olive oil
$\frac{1}{2}$ teaspoon salt
1 teaspoon sugar
About 20 grinds fresh black pepper
1 tablespoon whole grain mustard

Pull the lettuce leaves from the head, rinse
gently under cold water, and lay out on
clean towels to dry.

Use a spoon to remove the flesh in one
piece from each half of the avocado. Thinly
slice the avocado flesh into thin wedges.

Whisk together all the dressing ingredients.

Arrange the lettuce leaves on a plate and
top with the avocado wedges, scallions,
and cilantro. Finish with a healthy drizzling
of the dressing.

The easiest way to pit an avocado is with a chef's knife: Run the knife around the
avocado the long way from top to bottom (not the short way through the belly.) Stop
the knife when you run into the pit. Twist apart the avocado into two halves, then
whack the blade of the knife into the pit and give a quick twist to remove it. Now
you can use a spoon to easily remove the flesh from both halves of the avocado.

Shaved Zucchini and Radish Salad Over Smoked Salmon With Lemon-Dill Vinaigrette

Raw zucchini doesn't have a ton of flavor, but its texture
is really delicate, so it's perfect for this salad.

2 zucchini, rinsed and ends trimmed

4 ounces smoked salmon

1 bunch radishes, rinsed, tops and tails
    trimmed, and sliced as thinly as possible

Small handful dill fronds

For the Dressing

¼ cup extra-virgin olive oil

Juice of 2 lemons

1 small shallot, minced

2 teaspoons honey

15 to 20 grinds fresh black pepper

2 tablespoons finely chopped dill fronds

Use a peeler to shave the zucchini lengthwise on each side until you start to hit the
seedy middle part.

Lay a couple of pieces of smoked salmon in
the middle of a plate. Top the salmon layer
with a heap of shaved zucchini, radish
slices, and dill fronds.

Whisk the dressing ingredients together
until smooth. Drizzle the dressing over the
top of each salad.

Serves 4

Cantaloupe and Prosciutto With Ginger, Honey, and Mint

One of the classic combinations of fine dining is cantaloupe and prosciutto, and I'm a huge fan. But I thought it'd be fun to add some zing and a bit more sweetness to the mix.

1 medium cantaloupe
1 (2-inch) piece fresh ginger, peeled and
    finely grated into a small bowl
2 tablespoons honey
Small handful fresh mint, leaves torn
About ¼ pound prosciutto, thinly sliced

Cut the cantaloupe in half lengthwise and scoop out the seeds. Slice each half into 6 pieces and cut away the rinds. Cut each wedge in 3, leaving one end attached. Fan 2 of these sliced wedges on a plate. Scatter the ginger around the plate, drizzle with honey, and garnish with mint leaves. Place a couple of rolled prosciutto slices around the plate.

Fennel, Baby Arugula, and Green Apple Salad

This is one of my standby winter salads. In fact, if I have to cook in a new place and I'm unsure of the fresh greens I can get, I put this salad on the menu because you can get these ingredients consistently all year-round. If you can't find baby arugula, just use the regular kind.

For the Salad

1 cup walnut halves or pieces
1 small bulb fennel with top
1 Granny Smith apple
5 ounces baby arugula

For the Dressing

Juice of 1 lemon
Juice of 1 orange
2 tablespoons cider vinegar
2 teaspoons Dijon mustard
1 shallot, finely chopped
1 teaspoon sugar
$\frac{1}{2}$ teaspoon salt
$\frac{1}{3}$ cup extra-virgin olive oil

Preheat the oven to 350°F.

Lay the walnuts out on a baking sheet and bake in the oven about 7 minutes, until toasted and fragrant.

Cut the top away from the fennel bulb. Pinch off a small handful of the fronds, coarsely chop them, and reserve. Cut the fennel bulb in half lengthwise and carefully cut away the core.

Fill a large bowl with cold water. Slice the fennel crosswise as thinly as possible either with a chef's knife or a mandoline, and transfer to the water. Core the apple and slice the apple as thinly as possible. Add to the bowl with the fennel.

Whisk together the dressing ingredients or shake together well in a sealable container.

When all the elements of the salad are ready, strain the fennel and apples and lay out on a kitchen towel or paper towel to soak up the excess moisture. Toss with the arugula, then lay out on a serving platter. Pour the dressing over the top of the salad, then top with the walnuts and reserved fennel fronds.

Serves 6

Fennel turns brown if left out in the open for too long, so if you want to prepare it in advance, submerge it in a large dish of cold water and squeeze a lemon into the water.

Latin Cabbage and Corn Salad

When you get tired of eating leafy greens, this Latin-style salad
is a really nice option. The corn adds some sweet substance
as well as color contrast to the mix.

For the Dressing

½ cup olive oil
Juice of 2 limes
2 tablespoons red wine vinegar
1 teaspoon salt
1 teaspoon sugar
20 grinds fresh black pepper

For the Salad

1 pound white cabbage, shredded
1 pound red cabbage, shredded
1 (15-ounce) can corn kernels, drained
1 bunch cilantro, finely chopped
1 bunch scallions, thinly sliced

Make the dressing by whisking together all the ingredients.

Toss the salad ingredients together in a large mixing bowl.

Just before serving, toss the salad with the dressing.

Deconstructed Pan-Grilled Caesar

I first saw romaine lettuce grilled when I worked in a restaurant in Philadelphia. I thought that was just the coolest thing ever. So here's a classic that I find infinitely improved with a little help from the grill pan. Make sure to coat all the lettuce leaves with oil before grilling or else they will dry out and burn.

¼ cup extra-virgin olive oil
2 garlic cloves, finely chopped
Salt
Fresh black pepper
3 romaine lettuce hearts
½ lemon
Shaved Parmesan or pecorino Romano
Anchovy oil from a can of anchovies
    packed in olive oil
Handful fresh flat-leaf parsley leaves,
    chopped

Heat a grill pan over high heat.

For the salad, in a small bowl, combine the olive oil, garlic, a few pinches of salt, and about 15 grinds of pepper. Cut the lettuce hearts in half lengthwise and brush with the olive oil mixture.

Grill the lettuce until nicely blackened in places and semi-wilted. Grill in stages if your grill pan isn't large enough to grill in one stage. Transfer the lettuce to a serving platter.

Squeeze the lemon over the lettuce. Sprinkle the shaved Parmesan over the top, drizzle with the anchovy oil, and finish with the chopped parsley.

Roasted Squash, Spinach, and Leek Salad With Maple Syrup Dressing

I had this in mind as my ultimate winter salad because all the ingredients seem to scream "winter" and because it's a heartier salad than a lot of my others. Prepping and roasting the squash is a bit of extra work, but it also gives you a more substantial salad, one that could make a light meal on its own.

For the Salad

1 small butternut squash, peeled, seeded, and cut into 1½-inch cubes

Extra-virgin olive oil

Salt

1 cup pecan halves

1 small leek

10 ounces spinach, rinsed, dried, and large stems removed

For the Dressing

¼ cup pure maple syrup

¼ cup cider vinegar

⅓ cup olive oil

2 teaspoons Dijon mustard

1 shallot, minced

½ teaspoon salt

15 to 20 grinds fresh black pepper

Preheat the oven to 400°F.

Toss the squash cubes on a baking sheet with olive oil and salt. Roast 25 minutes,

until tender, tossing every 10 minutes or so. Remove the squash from the oven and allow to cool fully.

Spread the pecans out on another baking sheet and toast in the oven for 5 minutes.

Remove the green tops and bottom root from the leek. Cut the remaining portion of the leek in half lengthwise and rinse under cold water to wash away any grit inside the leek. Cut each half in half crosswise, then thinly cut vertically to create leek matchsticks.

Make the dressing by shaking together all the dressing ingredients in a sealable container or whisk together in a bowl. Toss the spinach with the dressing, divide the spinach between serving plates, and top with the squash pieces. Scatter the leek matchsticks around the salad, then finish with the toasted pecans.

I usually have good, real maple syrup lying around my pantry. It is on the expensive side, but you can usually find small containers of syrup that only cost a few bucks. By all means, do not substitute artificial pancake syrup. You're better off leaving it out altogether!

Dandelion Greens With Beet Dressing and Shaved Goat Gouda

It's pretty exciting that dandelion greens are widely available in supermarkets these days. They look beautiful, they're very hearty, and they have an interesting, slightly bitter flavor. To offset the bitterness, I turn to one of my favorite sweet standbys, beets. The beets also give the dressing an almost supernatural color. Got to love beets!

For the Salad

⅓ cup sliced almonds
2 bunches dandelion greens
¼ pound goat Gouda, shaved

For the Dressing

⅓ cup extra-virgin olive oil
2 tablespoons red wine vinegar
Juice of 1 lime
Juice of 1 lemon
1 pound boiled beets
Salt

Preheat the oven to 350°F.

Lay the almonds out on a baking sheet and toast 5 to 7 minutes, until golden brown.

Wash and trim the greens.

Combine the dressing ingredients in a blender container and blend until perfectly smooth. Spoon a generous amount onto a serving plate. Top with a small bunch of greens, then top with a small handful of toasted almond slices and the cheese shavings.

{ If you can't find goat Gouda, try ricotta salata. Parmesan works well too.

Arugula, Red Apple, and Radish Salad With Cider Vinaigrette and Goat Cheese

I love the color of the red apples and radishes in this salad. And apples and goat cheese are a match made in heaven.

For the Dressing

¼ cup cider vinegar
⅓ cup extra-virgin olive oil
2 teaspoons whole grain mustard
1 shallot, minced
Salt
Freshly ground black pepper

For the Salad

2 bunches arugula, thick stems removed, rinsed and dried
½ pound radishes, thinly sliced
1 red apple, unpeeled, cored and thinly sliced
4 ounces soft goat cheese, crumbled

In a small bowl, whisk together the vinegar, olive oil, mustard, shallot, and salt and pepper to taste. Toss the arugula, radishes, and red apple together in a salad bowl. Toss the salad with the dressing right before serving and season to taste with salt and pepper. Top with crumbled goat cheese.

{ Make sure your goat cheese is cold before you try to crumble or else it will just moosh up. Also, use two forks to crumble it instead of your hands

Buttery Baby Pea Soup With Pan-Grilled Bread, page 74

Soups

Soups are one of my favorite things to cook because they are so simple to make, yet they are full of flavor and they fill you up. I grew up knowing the virtues of good soup because my father would make his famous chicken noodle soup for the family every Friday night. It was the first thing out on the table, and it was so good I couldn't stop myself from having helping after helping. Of course, I then had no room for anything else, but that was okay—good soup was all I needed to be happy. Things really haven't changed that much.

I'm always surprised at just how flavorful soups are. I think it's because there is no flavor loss during the cooking process—everything that goes into the pot stays in the pot. That means all the nutrients too, which is why soups are really healthy for you, in addition to all their other virtues.

You can pretty much make soup out of anything, so trying to choose just a few soups to include here was no easy task. My goal was to give a wide variety of soups so there's something for everyone and something for every season. I also included a chilled soup for a refreshing start to a summer afternoon meal.

New England Clam Chowder

My mom has always loved New England clam chowder, and she passed her love on to me. Even though it's traditionally a winter soup, it was a summer tradition for me and my mom when we'd go to the beach in Massachusetts for the summer. Now I just eat it all year round!

3 tablespoons vegetable oil

1 medium onion, finely diced

3 celery stalks (tender leaves reserved), trimmed and quartered lengthwise, then sliced into ¼-inch pieces

3 tablespoons all-purpose flour

2 cups chicken or vegetable stock

2 (6½-ounce) cans chopped clams in juice

1 cup heavy cream

2 bay leaves

1 pound Idaho potatoes, cut into ½-inch cubes

Salt and freshly ground black pepper

Heat the oil in a large pot over medium-high heat. Add the onion and celery and sauté until softened, mixing often. Stir in the flour and stir to distribute evenly. Add the stock, clams and juice, cream, bay leaves, and potatoes and stir to combine. Bring to a simmer, stirring consistently (the mixture will thicken), then reduce the heat to medium-low and cook 20 minutes, stirring often, until the potatoes are tender. Season to taste with salt and pepper.

Ladle into serving bowls and garnish with reserved celery leaves.

Serves 6–8

Butternut Squash and Pear Soup

This is the ultimate fall soup. I break it out in October and make it through the winter. Of course, you can get these ingredients year-round, but I like to save it for the cooler months.

4 tablespoons (½ stick) unsalted butter

2 large onions, diced

1 medium butternut squash, peeled, seeded, and cut into 1-inch pieces

4 medium fragrant Bosc, Anjou, or Comice pears, peeled; 3 chopped into 1-inch pieces and 1 diced finely for garnish

1 quart reduced-sodium chicken or vegetable stock

2 rosemary sprigs

½ cup heavy cream

Salt

Freshly ground black pepper

Sugar

Heat the butter in a large pot over medium heat until melted and bubbling. Add the onions and cook until softened and starting to turn translucent. Add the squash and pears and cook 5 minutes. Add the stock. The ingredients should be submerged in liquid. If not, add just enough water to do so. Add the rosemary, bring to a simmer, and cook until the squash and pears are very tender, about 45 minutes. Remove the rosemary sprigs. Purée right in the pot with an immersion blender till smooth, or in batches in a blender. Season with salt, pepper, and sugar to taste. Place a heap of diced pear in the middle of each serving bowl, then surround with soup.

Serves 8–10

Buttery Baby Pea Soup With Pan-Grilled Bread

This soup couldn't be simpler—it only has four ingredients.
But it needs nothing more—it's perfect just the way it is.

For the Soup

1 pound frozen green peas

4 tablespoons (½ stick) unsalted butter

1 (14½-ounce) can reduced-sodium chicken
or vegetable stock

1 small onion, roughly chopped

Salt and freshly ground black pepper to
taste

For the Bread

Extra-virgin olive oil

1 small loaf dense rustic bread, cut into
½-inch slices

Salt

Combine all the soup ingredients in a medium pot. The peas should be submerged in liquid. If they aren't, add just enough water to top them off. Bring to a simmer over medium heat and simmer about 10 minutes, until the onions are soft enough to purée but the peas are still nice and green.

While the peas are cooking, grill the bread. Heat a grill pan over high heat for 5 minutes. Pour some olive oil onto a large plate. Sprinkle the oil with salt, then dip pieces of bread quickly into the oil on both sides. Grill the bread until well browned, even blackened in some places, on both sides, about 3 to 4 minutes per side.

With an immersion blender, standing blender, or food processor, purée the soup to a smooth consistency. Ladle into serving bowls and serve with the grilled bread.

Serves 6–8

74

Moroccan Spiced Chickpea Soup

Chickpeas seem to call out for Moroccan spices, so that's what they get here.
I make this soup really chunky and hearty.

3 tablespoons extra-virgin olive oil, plus
   more for drizzling
1 large onion, cut into medium dice
4 garlic cloves , finely chopped
1 teaspoon ground cinnamon
1 teaspoon ground cumin
¼ teaspoon cayenne pepper
1 teaspoon sweet paprika
1 cup canned chopped tomatoes
3 (15-ounce) cans chickpeas, drained
1 quart reduced-sodium chicken or
   vegetable stock
2 teaspoons sugar
Salt
Freshly ground black pepper
2 tablespoons unsalted butter
1 (2½-ounce) package prewashed baby
   spinach

Heat the olive oil in a large pot over
medium-high heat. Sauté the onion and
garlic until the onion begins to turn
translucent; lower the heat if browning
starts to occur. Add the spices and sauté a
minute or so. Add the tomatoes, chickpeas,
stock, sugar, a couple of pinches of salt,
and 10 grinds of fresh pepper. Stir well.
The chickpeas should be just covered with
liquid. If the level is shy, add some water so
the chickpeas are just covered. Bring to a
simmer, then lower the heat to low and
gently simmer 45 minutes to an hour. Stir

in the butter. Remove the soup from the
heat. Use a potato masher to mash up
some of the chickpeas right in the pot. Stir
in the spinach until wilted, just a couple of
minutes. Season again to taste with salt
and pepper.

Portion the soup into bowls and drizzle
lightly with extra-virgin olive oil.

Serves 8–10

Pumpkin and Chipotle Corn Chowder

This is great to make in the fall when pumpkins are plentiful. If you can't find pumpkin other times of the year, just substitute butternut squash or another sweet, orange-fleshed squash. The smokiness and heat of the chipotles is perfect for such a hearty stew, and is nicely balanced by its creaminess.

3 tablespoons unsalted butter or
    vegetable oil
Flesh from a 3- to 4-pound pumpkin, cut
    into 1-inch cubes
1 large onion, diced
3 tablespoons all-purpose flour
1 quart reduced-sodium chicken stock
½ pound frozen corn kernels
2 chipotle peppers, roughly chopped
½ cup heavy cream
5 thyme sprigs
Salt and freshly ground black pepper
1 small bunch cilantro, stems removed and
    leaves roughly chopped

Heat the butter or oil in a large pot over medium heat. Add the pumpkin and onion and cook 5 minutes. Add the flour and stir into the onion and pumpkin. Gradually add the chicken stock, stirring all the while. Add the corn, chipotle peppers, cream, and thyme and bring to a simmer. Reduce the heat to low and simmer about 20 minutes, or until the pumpkin is fork-tender but not falling apart. Remove from the heat and season to taste with salt and pepper. Stir in most of the cilantro leaves, reserving some for garnish. Ladle the soup into serving bowls and garnish with the remaining cilantro leaves.

Serves 8–10

Asian Mushroom Soup

This is a fresh and light soup, but because of the mushrooms,
it's still very satisfying.

2 quarts reduced-sodium chicken broth

3 tablespoons soy sauce

2 tablespoons fish sauce (optional)

1 (2-inch) piece fresh ginger, peeled and
thinly sliced

2 shallots, peeled and thinly sliced

5 ounces cremini mushrooms, thinly sliced

10 small shiitake mushrooms, cleaned and
left whole

Outer leaves of 1 small napa cabbage or
½ large cabbage, leaves roughly torn

2 carrots, peeled, cut in half lengthwise,
then in half crosswise, and very thinly
sliced

2 good handfuls snow peas

1 small bunch scallions, thinly sliced

Dark sesame oil

Combine the broth, soy sauce, fish sauce, if using, ginger, and shallots in a large saucepan or stockpot. Heat over medium heat and bring to a simmer. Add the remaining ingredients except the snow peas, scallions, and sesame oil. Simmer 30 minutes, then add the snow peas. Cook just a few minutes longer, until the snow peas have softened slightly but are still bright green. Add the scallions to the pot, remove from the heat, and ladle into serving bowls. Drizzle a bit of sesame oil over the top of each serving.

Serves 8–10

You can juse a peeler to thinly "slice" the carrots once you've trimmed and peeled them. Just use plenty of pressure.

Shrimp and Spicy Sausage Stew

This is a relative of a gumbo, but thicker and not so heavily spiced. I like the mild flavors of the white wine and thyme to be able to shine through.

3/4 pound spicy sausage

3 tablespoons unsalted butter

1 medium onion, finely diced

3 garlic cloves , minced

3 tablespoons all-purpose flour

1 teaspoon ground cumin

2 teaspoons paprika

1 quart reduced-sodium chicken stock

1/2 cup white wine

1 cup chopped tomatoes

15 grinds fresh black pepper

6 fresh thyme sprigs

15 shrimp, peeled and deveined

Heat a large skillet over medium-high heat. Brown the sausage links as fully as possible on all sides. Remove and set aside to cool.

Reduce the heat to medium, melt the butter in the pan, and wait for it to start bubbling. Add the onion and garlic, and sauté until the onion has softened and turns translucent. Add the flour, cumin, and paprika, and stir into the onion and garlic until the mixture becomes dry. Add the stock, white wine, and tomatoes and stir to incorporate well. Season with the black pepper and add the thyme sprigs. Bring the mixture to a simmer and cook at a low simmer for 15 minutes.

Slice the sausage on an angle into 1/2-inch slices and add to the pot. Add the shrimp and cook 5 minutes longer.

Serves 6–8

{ When you cook the sausage for the first time and then set it aside, it's not supposed to be cooked through fully, it's just supposed to be browned nicely on the outside. The sausage will cook fully once you add it to the simmering liquid.

Plum-Ginger Glazed Chicken With Cauliflower-Parsnip Mash, page 100

Poultry

When I go to restaurants, it seems as if some chefs have almost forgotten about that wonderful, humble bird, the chicken. I know it's common, but it didn't become popular without reason. It's delicious, and so versatile. There's really no end to how you can cook a chicken. Whole, in pieces, chicken will go in whatever flavor direction you want to take it. The same goes for turkey, although turkey can require a bit more tender loving care to get it tender and moist. But when done right, turkey may take the prize as my favorite bird. To demonstrate poultry's versatility, I've come up with a bunch of recipes that run the gamut in terms of flavor, textures, and regional influences. Poultry also happens to be one of the least expensive proteins in the market. Dark meat is cheaper than white meat, which I've never been able to figure out because dark meat is so much tastier. So on counts of both taste and expense, I use dark meat over white meat as often as possible. Dark meat is most delicious when you cook it long and slow, as I do in my creamy chicken thigh dish. But white meat lovers out there, don't fret—almost all of my other recipes include white meat.

Braised Dark Meat Turkey
Over Egg Noodles

Dark meat turkey is way underutilized even though it is so readily available, inexpensive, and delicious. Here, after cooking it for a while in a really tasty, savory stewing brew, it just falls apart and melds with the sauce to make the most amazing topping for egg noodles. And egg noodles are another one of my all-time favorites. My father used to make them almost every week and he would serve them with chicken soup.

Salt and freshly ground black pepper
4 to 5 pounds turkey wings and drumsticks
¼ cup vegetable oil
1 large onion, cut into ½-inch dice
4 carrots, peeled, halved lengthwise, and
    cut into ½-inch dice
4 celery stalks, bottoms and tips
    trimmed, halved lengthwise, and
    cut into ½-inch dice
6 ounces tomato paste
1 cup reduced-sodium chicken broth
¼ cup cider vinegar
12 ounces ale or good lager beer
6 to 8 garlic cloves, peeled and smashed
1 cup pitted oil-cured olives
2 large fresh rosemary sprigs
Cooked egg noodles, for serving

Generously salt and pepper the turkey.

Heat 2 tablespoons oil in a large heavy pot or Dutch oven over high heat. Add the turkey wings and drumsticks and brown as evenly as possible all over. Do this in batches if necessary.

Once browned, remove the turkey from the pot. Reduce the heat to medium-high, add the remaining oil, the onion, carrots, and celery, and cook until tender. Add the tomato paste and cook, stirring, until it is mixed in. Then add all the remaining ingredients, except the olives and rosemary, and stir until everything is incorporated. Bring to a simmer, then add the turkey back to the pot, along with the olives and rosemary, and bring to a simmer again. Cook about 3 to 3½ hours, partially covered, over a low flame at a low simmer until the turkey meat falls off the bone easily with just a little nudge from a fork. Remove the rosemary sprigs and serve over hot egg noodles.

Serves 6

Check occasionally during cooking to see if the turkey is getting too browned or dried where it is not submerged under the braising liquid. If so, stir into the liquid and continue cooking.

Chicken Breast Scaloppine With Lemon-Caper Sauce and Garlic-Sautéed Spinach

Making scaloppine is a fantastic way to get a lot out of meat cutlets. By cutting the cutlets down and pounding them thin, you can get twice as many portions out of the meat. The pounding part is pretty fun, too. The sauce and spinach are the classic accompaniments.

For the Spinach

10 ounces curly, whole leaf spinach, rinsed
    and large stems plucked
3 tablespoons extra-virgin olive oil
3 to 4 garlic cloves, thinly sliced
Salt

For the Chicken

2 boneless, skinless chicken breasts,
    about 1½ pounds total
⅓ cup all-purpose flour
1 teaspoon salt
15 grinds fresh black pepper
Olive oil
⅓ cup white wine
2 tablespoons capers
1 tablespoon unsalted butter
½ lemon

Make the spinach: Bring a large pot of salted water to a boil. Throw in the spinach and let it wilt for 30 seconds to a minute, then remove to a strainer.

Heat the olive oil in a large skillet over high heat. Add the garlic and sauté for 30 seconds to a minute, but don't brown. Add the strained, wilted spinach and toss in the hot oil and garlic. Cook until hot but not so much that the spinach loses its dark green freshness. Season with salt to taste. Keep warm while you prepare the chicken.

Cut the chicken breasts in half lengthwise. Pound each slice with a heavy saucepan (or meat mallet, if you have one) between two sheets of plastic wrap until they are half as thick.

Combine the flour, salt, and pepper and mix thoroughly. Dredge each piece of chicken in the flour mixture until fully and evenly coated.

Heat ¼ cup olive oil in a nonstick skillet over high heat until smoking. Add the chicken pieces and fry just until lightly browned on both sides. The thin pieces of chicken will cook quickly, so be careful not to overcook.

Remove the chicken from the pan and set aside. Add the wine to the pan and reduce by half. Add the capers and butter and cook another minute or so, until the butter has melted and the mixture has slightly thickened.

Pour the sauce over the chicken and finish with a squeeze of lemon over each piece. Serve with the garlic-sautéed spinach.

Serves 4

Chicken Tikka Masala
With Cardamom Basmati Rice

Whenever my friends and I order takeout from the great local Indian restaurant on the corner, this dish is on the list. But you may not have access to my great local Indian restaurant on the corner, so I've replicated it for you here.

1½ pounds boneless, skinless chicken breasts
1 cup plain whole milk yogurt
3 large garlic cloves, pressed
1 (1-inch) piece fresh ginger, peeled and grated
1 teaspoon ground cinnamon
¼ teaspoon cayenne pepper
3 teaspoons sweet paprika
10 cardamom pods, cracked lightly with the back of a chef's knife
2 tablespoons honey
1½ teaspoons salt
20 grinds fresh black pepper
3 tablespoons unsalted butter
1 medium onion, finely chopped
2 tablespoons curry powder
1 6-ounce can tomato paste
1 cup heavy cream

For the Rice

2 cups water
2 tablespoons unsalted butter
8 to 10 whole cardamom pods
Salt
1 cup basmati rice

Cut the chicken breasts roughly into 2 × 2-inch cubes. In a large bowl, mix together the yogurt, garlic, ginger, cinnamon, cayenne, paprika, cardamom, honey, salt, and pepper until thoroughly combined. Add the chicken pieces to the yogurt mixture, cover, and refrigerate at least 1 hour or as long as overnight, but bring to room temperature before cooking.

Make the rice: Combine the water, butter, cardamom pods, and a few pinches of salt in a saucepan and bring to a boil. Add the rice, stir, then cover and reduce the heat to low. Cook 20 minutes, until the rice is fluffy.

In a large skillet, heat the butter over medium-high heat. Add the onion and cook until translucent. Stir in the curry powder, then the tomato paste, and cook a couple of minutes. Add the cream and mix together until smooth. Slide in the chicken and marinade, stir well, and bring to a simmer. Reduce the heat so the liquid remains at a low simmer. Cook about 15 minutes, until the chicken is cooked through but still tender and moist. The mixture should also thicken. Serve over the basmati rice.

Serves 4–6

Roasted Chorizo and Sun-Dried Tomato Chicken Over Rosemary Black Beans

It's important to use sun-dried tomatoes packed in olive oil, otherwise they'll really dry out during roasting. You can protect the chorizo and tomatoes from drying out too much by tucking them underneath the chicken.

For the Chicken

Two 3-pound roasting chickens, cut in half
Salt and freshly ground black pepper
3 tablespoons olive oil
20 garlic cloves, lightly smashed and skins removed
6 rosemary sprigs
1 cup sun-dried tomatoes marinated in olive oil
¼ pound dried chorizo, sliced into ¼-inch pieces

For the Beans

2 tablespoons vegetable oil
1 medium onion, diced
2 (15.5-ounce) cans black beans (frijoles negros), rinsed
1 cup chicken stock
2 rosemary sprigs
2 tablespoons unsalted butter
Salt and freshly ground black pepper

Preheat the oven to 375°F.

Heat the oil in a saucepan over medium-high heat. Sauté the onion until it softens and starts to turn translucent. Add the beans, stock, and rosemary. Bring to a simmer, reduce the heat, and simmer 10 minutes. Stir in the butter, season with salt and pepper to taste, and cook 5 minutes longer.

Place the chicken on a baking sheet, season lightly with salt and pepper to taste on all sides, then add remaining ingredients. Toss to coat, distributing the ingredients evenly over and around the chicken.

Bake 35 to 40 minutes, until the skin is crispy brown and the juices at the thigh joint run clear when pierced.

Spoon beans onto plate and top with chicken and roasted chorizo and sun-dried tomatoes.

Serves 6–8

Creamy Chicken Thighs and Mushrooms Over Gemelli

Chicken thighs are one of the great supermarket finds. They are one of the most inexpensive pieces of meat in the market and one of the tastiest. This dish has an ethereal quality to it because it is so pale, but don't let looks deceive: It's full of complex, layered flavors. I find the dense, slightly chewy texture of gemelli pasta the perfect complement, but if you can't find gemelli use whatever small, dense cut of pasta you can find.

3 tablespoons vegetable oil
2 pounds chicken thighs, skin and excess
    fat removed
Salt and freshly ground black pepper
1 medium onion, finely chopped
3 celery stalks, sliced (about 1 cup)
¼ cup all-purpose flour
1 cup white wine
1 quart reduced-sodium chicken stock
1 cup heavy cream
2 large bay leaves
12 ounces white button mushrooms,
    brushed clean and stems trimmed
1 pound gemelli, cooked until al dente
Chopped fresh parsley

Heat the oil in a large pot over medium-high heat. Season the chicken generously with salt and pepper to taste. Brown the chicken on both sides. Remove the chicken when browned and reserve. Add the onion and celery and sauté until softened, 5 to 7 minutes. Stir in the flour until evenly distributed. Gradually stir in the wine, chicken stock, and cream. Add the bay leaves, chicken, and mushrooms. Bring the mixture to a simmer, reduce the heat to low, cover the pot, and simmer for 2 hours.

Serve over cooked gemelli and garnish with parsley.

Serves 6–8

Herbes de Provence Roasted Chicken With Lemon and Garlic and Fennel-Stewed Lentils

This is an homage to peasant, provençal cooking. Luckily herbes de Provence, the classic mixture of herbs indigenous to southern France, can be found right on your supermarket shelf. The most distinctive part of the mixture is the inclusion of lavender buds, which add a beautiful perfume to the roasted chicken. The fennel lentils are a perfect complement. Make sure you get the small green lentils, though, because the larger varieties cook slightly differently.

For the Chicken

1 (3- to 4-pound) roasting chicken
Salt and freshly ground black pepper
Extra-virgin olive oil
¼ cup herbes de Provence
1 lemon, cut into eighths
8 garlic cloves, smashed

For the Lentils

3 tablespoons vegetable oil
1 medium onion, diced
½ pound carrots, peeled and diced
1 small fennel bulb (½ to ¾ pound), bottom
    and core removed and thinly sliced
3 cups reduced-sodium chicken stock
2 bay leaves
1½ cups small green lentils
Salt and freshly ground black pepper

Preheat oven to 375°F.

Season the chicken generously with salt and pepper to taste. Drizzle generously with olive oil. Scatter the herbs over the chicken and use your hands to rub them all over.

Stuff most of the lemon and garlic into the cavity of the chicken. Scatter the rest over the top and press into the chicken so they don't fall off during the cooking process.

Roast 1 hour 10 minutes for a 3-pound chicken, 1 hour 20 minutes for a 4-pound chicken.

Heat the vegetable oil in a large stockpot or Dutch oven over medium-high heat. Sauté the onion and carrots until the onion starts to soften. Add the fennel and sauté until fennel starts to soften. Add the stock and bay leaves and bring to a vigorous simmer. Add the lentils, bring back to a simmer, cover, and cook 30 minutes. Season to taste with salt and pepper.

Serves 6

Jerk Chicken
With Banana Fried Rice

This is fun to make because you get to use the blender to purée
all the marinade ingredients and you get to take advantage of your oven broiler.
The broiler is a great way to get the blackening typical of the islands while evenly
cooking the meat. Frying the bananas for the rice makes for addictively sweet
rice, but using green bananas is important because ripe bananas
will turn to mush almost instantaneously in the pan.

For the Marinade

2 tablespoons vegetable oil

Zest and juice of 1 large lime

5 garlic cloves, roughly chopped

1 jalapeño, seeded and roughly chopped

1 (2-inch) piece ginger, peeled and roughly
   chopped

2 tablespoons fresh thyme leaves

2 tablespoons ground allspice

2 tablespoons ground cinnamon

2 tablespoons dried oregano

1 tablespoon sugar

2 teaspoons salt

35 grinds fresh black pepper

For the Chicken

1 (3- to 4-pound) chicken, cut into pieces

For the Fried Banana Rice

5 tablespoons vegetable oil

2 green bananas, cut into $\frac{1}{2}$-inch slices

2 teaspoons sugar

1 medium onion, diced

$\frac{1}{2}$ teaspoon ground cinnamon

1 cup rice, cooked

Salt

Place all the chicken marinade ingredients
in a blender and blend until smooth and
thick.

Place the chicken pieces in a large bowl,
pour the marinade over the top of the
chicken, cover the bowl with plastic wrap,
and refrigerate for at least 1 hour and as
long as overnight, the longer the better.

Preheat the broiler and set the rack to the
middle setting.

Lay the marinated chicken pieces on a baking or broiler pan, skin-side up.

continued

Jerk Chicken With Banana Fried Rice *(continued)*

Broil 20 minutes, then turn over and broil 10 minutes longer.

Heat 2 tablespoons of the oil for a couple of minutes in a large skillet over high heat. In a bowl, toss the bananas with the sugar to coat. Add the banana slices to the hot oil and cook on each side until nicely browned but not mushy. Remove the bananas and set aside on a plate. Add the remaining 3 tablespoons of oil to the pan, allow to heat

for 1 minute, then add the onion. Sauté a few minutes until the onion is softened and translucent. Season with the cinnamon. Add the cooked rice to the onion and cook until heated through, stirring constantly. Toss the bananas into the hot rice and season to taste with salt.

Serves 6

Orange and Five-Spice Roasted Chicken With Sweet Potato Smash

Five-spice powder screams for sweet elements, which is
why I pair it with oranges and sweet potatoes.

For the Chicken

1 (3- to 4-pound) chicken, cut into pieces
1 large navel orange
Olive oil
5 tablespoons five-spice powder
10 dashes red pepper flakes
Salt and freshly ground black pepper

For the Sweet Potato Smash

2 pounds sweet potatoes or yams, peeled
   and cut into 2-inch chunks
4 tablespoons ($\frac{1}{2}$ stick) unsalted butter
1 large onion, finely chopped
Salt

Preheat the oven to 375°F.

Put the cut-up chicken in a roasting sheet
or broiler pan. Slice the orange into $\frac{1}{2}$-inch
slices and squeeze over the top of the
chicken and toss in the rinds. Drizzle 2
tablespoons olive oil over the chicken, then
add the remaining ingredients. Toss vigorously until the chicken pieces are fully
coated with the spices.

Bake for 45 minutes, or until the chicken
is well browned, the orange slices have
withered, and the chicken juices run clear
when a piece of chicken is cut at its thickest part.

In a large pot, submerge the potatoes in
cold water. Bring to a boil, cook until the
potatoes are fork-tender, about 20 minutes, and strain well. In a skillet, heat the
butter over medium-high heat. Sauté the
onion until translucent, then add to the potatoes. Mash the potatoes together with
the onion until a rough mash forms. Season to taste with salt.

Serve the chicken with the sweet potato
smash.

Serves 4–6

Plum-Ginger Glazed Chicken With Cauliflower-Parsnip Mash

Plum and ginger are a classic combination in Asian cooking. I think rosemary adds something nice to the mix. And the sugars from the plum preserves make for sticky, caramelized chicken skin that's simply irresistible.

For the Cauliflower-Parsnip Mash

1 large head cauliflower, about 2 pounds
2 large parsnips, about 1 pound, peeled and
    ends trimmed
6 garlic cloves, peeled and smashed
½ cup white wine
⅓ cup heavy cream
Salt
Freshly ground black pepper

For the Chicken

1 (3- to 4-pound) chicken, cut into pieces
Salt
Freshly ground black pepper
6 ounces (¾ cup) plum preserves
1 (1-inch) piece fresh ginger, peeled and
    grated
2 tablespoons olive oil
4 to 5 fresh rosemary sprigs
15 peeled garlic cloves, lightly smashed
2 fresh plums, pitted and sliced into
    sixteenths

Preheat oven to 375°F.

Remove the stem and hard core from the cauliflower. Cut the cauliflower into medium-size florets. Cut the parsnips into 2-inch cubes. Place the cauliflower and parsnips in a baking dish large enough to hold them comfortably. Toss with the remaining ingredients and cover tightly with aluminum foil. Bake 45 minutes. Transfer to a large mixing bowl and mash well. Reheat on the stovetop before serving.

Lay the chicken pieces on a baking sheet or broiler pan. Season generously with a few pinches of salt and about 25 grinds of fresh black pepper. Add the remaining ingredients. Toss ingredients together so that the chicken pieces are fully coated with the preserves.

Bake for 40 minutes, or until the chicken is beautifully browned and the chicken juices run clear when a piece of chicken is cut at its thickest part. Serve with Cauliflower-Parsnip Mash.

Serves 4–6

Lemon Brined Turkey
With Sourdough Bread Stuffing and
Orange-Fennel Cranberry Sauce

Here's the perfect Thanksgiving meal or the fix you need to satisfy
the gobble-gobble cravings other times of the year.

For the Brine

2 gallons water

1 cup sugar

1 cup kosher salt

2 lemons, halved

4 bay leaves

3 cinnamon sticks

Small handful cloves

1 (12- to 15-pound) turkey

Combine all the brine ingredients in a container or pot large enough to hold the turkey. Make sure all the sugar and salt have been fully dissolved. Add the turkey and refrigerate about 6 hours or overnight.

Preheat the oven to 350°F.

Remove the turkey from the brine and transfer to a roasting pan with a rack. Stuff the turkey with the lemon halves, bay leaves, and cinnamon sticks used in the brine. Cook the turkey for about 3½ hours, basting every 40 minutes or so. If any part of the turkey gets too brown toward the end of cooking, shield with pieces of aluminum foil. When the turkey is done, the juices should run clear from the breast and the legs should pull away from the bird easily. Remove from the heat and let rest for 15 minutes before carving.

Sourdough Bread Stuffing

1 (1-pound) loaf sourdough bread

8 tablespoons (1 stick) unsalted butter

10 ounces cremini mushrooms, sliced ½ inch
   thick in both directions

Salt

2 to 4 celery stalks with leaves, halved
   lengthwise and sliced

1 medium onion, chopped

About 10 fresh thyme sprigs, leaves
   stripped from the stems

10 to 12 fresh sage leaves, chopped

3½ cups reduced-sodium chicken broth

Freshly ground black pepper

3 tablespoons chopped Italian parsley
   leaves

continued

Sourdough Bread Stuffing *(continued)*

Preheat the oven to 350°F. Grease a 2-quart baking dish and set aside.

Cut or tear the bread into 1-inch cubes and spread it evenly on two baking sheets. Toast the bread in the oven until completely dry and beginning to crisp and brown, about 20 minutes. Transfer to a large mixing bowl.

Melt 2 tablespoons of butter in a large skillet over medium-high heat. Add the mushrooms and a few pinches of salt and sauté, stirring occasionally, until golden brown, about 6 to 8 minutes. Add the remaining butter, the celery, onion, and thyme. Cook, stirring frequently, until the vegetables have softened, about 5 minutes. Add the sage and the chicken broth to the skillet and stir to combine. Season with salt and pepper to taste.

Transfer the toasted bread cubes to a large bowl. Pour the chicken broth mixture over the bread cubes and toss to combine until the bread cubes absorb the liquid. Pour the mixture into the greased baking dish and sprinkle with parsley. Bake until heated through and the top is golden brown, about 40 minutes.

Fennel-Orange Cranberry Sauce

8 ounces frozen or fresh whole cranberries
½ navel orange, zested
Juice of 1 whole navel orange
½ cup sugar
½ cup water
½ teaspoon fennel seeds

Combine all the ingredients in a saucepan over medium heat. Bring to a simmer, then reduce the heat to low and cook, stirring frequently, until the cranberries begin to break down and the water evaporates, about 8 to 10 minutes. Remove from the heat and allow to cool before serving.

Serves 8

Seared Snapper Over Succotash, page 107

Fish

Alot of people tell me they are afraid to cook fish. Fish is really one of the simplest things to cook because the best way to cook fish is to do as little as possible to it. Good fresh fish has subtle, delicate flavors and textures, so you don't want to overcook or overseason it. Fish is probably the quickest protein to cook—most fish are done just a couple of minutes after they hit the pan. Of course, the flip side is sensitive, so you have to watch it and be careful. But that's not hard to do. As long as you pay attention to what's happening on the stove, you'll be fine. Unless you're cooking to rare or medium rare (in the case of tuna, for example), you can tell when white fish is done because the meat will separate or "flake" very easily. Most fish also turns from translucent to opaque.

If you don't cook fish often, this is a great time to get into it. Now more than ever, there's a great variety of fresh fish available at the supermarket fish counter. But there are still some laggards in the fish department, so try to go to a market that does a lot of business because that will mean their inventory is fresh. You can also tell fresh fish from giving it a quick look-see. The flesh should be intact and look firm, and its skin should glisten. Any fish that's browning, gray, or falling apart is a fish you want to stay away from. If you're buying whole fish, look for shiny skin and bright, clear, and shiny eyes.

Seared Snapper Over Succotash

Seared white fish, such as snapper, has such delicate, subtle flavor that you have to pair it with something very mild. Hence this succotash. It's flavorful, but it still lets the fish shine. I love the contrast of textures between the crispy fried fish and the creamy succotash laden with veggies.

For the Succotash

2 tablespoons unsalted butter

1 small onion, chopped

1 red bell pepper, stemmed, seeded, and diced

1 cup frozen baby lima beans

1 cup frozen corn kernels

1 cup light or heavy cream

1 teaspoon salt

Freshly ground black pepper

1 tablespoon finely chopped fresh sage

1 tablespoon finely chopped fresh parsley

For the Snapper

4 small red snapper fillets, with the skin on

Salt and freshly ground black pepper

2 teaspoons smoked or sweet paprika

2 tablespoons vegetable oil

Heat the butter in a large skillet over medium heat. Add the onion and red pepper and cook until softened, about 5 minutes. Add the lima beans, corn, cream, salt, and pepper to taste. Bring to a simmer and cook about 7 minutes, until the beans and corn are tender and the mixture has thickened slightly. Stir in the sage and parsley before serving.

Score the skin of the fish with a sharp paring knife without cutting into the flesh. Season the flesh side with salt and pepper to taste and sprinkle lightly with the paprika.

Heat the oil over high heat in a skillet. Sear the flesh side until well browned, about 3 to 4 minutes. Then flip and sear till the skin is crisp, 2 to 3 minutes.

Serve the fish over the succotash, skin-side up.

Serves 4

"Scrod" With Bay Shrimp Stuffing and Garlic-Sautéed Jerusalem Artichokes

Here in the Northeast, scrod just means the inexpensive white fish catch of the day. Cod, haddock, and pollock are what I come across most often. And because they all have similar textures and cooking times, this recipe works for all of them. Thickness can vary on these fish, so use cooking time here as a guide and just check to make sure the fish is tender and flaky before you remove it from the oven. If you can't find Jerusalem artichokes, use small Yukon gold potatoes instead.

For the Fish

1/2 pound cooked bay shrimp, finely chopped

4 tablespoons (1/2 stick) butter, melted, plus 1 tablespoon butter

Juice and zest of 1/2 lemon

2 tablespoons bread crumbs

Salt and freshly ground black pepper

2 (6-ounce) skinless, boneless cod, haddock, or pollock fillets

For the Jerusalem Artichokes

3 tablespoons extra-virgin olive oil

1/2 pound Jerusalem artichokes or "sunchokes," peeled and cut into 1/4-inch slices

5 garlic cloves, smashed

Few thyme sprigs, a couple reserved for garnish

Salt and freshly ground black pepper

Preheat oven to 325°F.

In a mixing bowl, stir the chopped shrimp, melted butter, and lemon juice. Add the bread crumbs and season lightly with salt and pepper.

Line a baking sheet with aluminum foil. Cut the unmelted butter into 3 even pats. Use one pat to grease the foil. Place half the filling in the center of the skinned side of each fillet and fold the fish over the filling to enclose. Place, opening-side down, on the baking sheet. Season the top of each stuffed fillet lightly with salt and pepper to taste. Top with a pat of butter.

Bake the fish for 30 minutes.

While the fish is cooking, make the Jerusalem artichokes: Heat the olive oil in a saucepan over medium-high heat for a minute or two. Add the chokes, garlic, and thyme, season with salt and pepper to taste, and sauté 5 minutes, or until fork-tender and the garlic is golden. Toss often to ensure even cooking.

Divide the chokes and garlic between two plates, spreading them around the center of the plate. Place a piece of fish in the middle of the plate. Garnish with the lemon zest and thyme sprigs.

Serves 2

Haddock Puttanesca
With Seared Fingerling Potatoes

This is a classic Italian sauce with rich, briny flavors. It's
the perfect thing to flavor flaky white haddock. And it's also one
of the easiest, fastest one-pot, stovetop meals.

For the Puttanesca Sauce

3 tablespoons extra virgin olive oil

4 large garlic cloves, thinly sliced

Few dashes red pepper flakes

$\frac{1}{2}$ cup white wine

1 (26-ounce) can chopped tomatoes

2 teaspoons finely chopped anchovies or
   anchovy paste (optional)

$\frac{1}{4}$ cup capers

2 handfuls pitted large green or black
   olives, quartered lengthwise

Salt and freshly ground black pepper

About 1$\frac{1}{2}$ pounds haddock fillet, cut into
   portion-size pieces

1 small bunch basil leaves, rinsed and stems
   removed

For the Potatoes

1 pound fingerling potatoes

2 tablespoons olive oil

Make the Puttanesca sauce: Heat the olive oil in a large skillet over medium-high heat. Add the garlic and red pepper flakes and cook just a minute. Pour in the wine and tomatoes, and bring to a simmer. Add the anchovies, if using, capers, and olives and simmer 10 minutes longer. Season sauce to taste with salt and pepper. Slide in the fish pieces, making sure they are submerged in sauce, and simmer 10 minutes longer. For the last couple of minutes of cooking, add the basil leaves so they wilt but don't lose their fresh appearance or flavor.

Place the fingerlings in a saucepan full of cold, salted water. Bring to a boil and cook about 15 minutes, until you can pierce them through with a fork (but they should still be snappy). Strain the potatoes and run under cold water. Once the potatoes have cooled down, cut them in half lengthwise. Heat the olive oil in a large skillet over high heat. Add the potatoes, cut-side down, and cook until well browned, about 5 minutes.

Serve the potatoes alongside the fish.

Serves 4–6

110

Citrus Grilled Tuna Steak
Over Panzanella-Niçoise Salad

This is a confused salad, but confusion can be delicious. It's a
vibrant cross between the classic Italian bread and tomato salad and the
traditional salad from the famous French city. I make the dressing for
the salad pretty wet so the toasted bread can soak it up.

For the Fish

2 (4-ounce) fresh tuna steaks
Salt and freshly ground black pepper
Olive oil
Zest of 1 lime, 1 lemon, and 1 orange

For the Dressing

⅓ cup extra-virgin olive oil
1 large shallot, finely chopped
3 tablespoons red wine vinegar
Juice of 1 lime, 1 lemon, and 1 small orange
1 teaspoon salt
15 grinds fresh black pepper

For the Salad

1½ pounds plum tomatoes, cored, seeded,
    and cut into ½-inch pieces
1 small bunch fresh mint leaves,
    finely chopped
1 small bunch fresh parsley leaves,
    finely chopped
1 small bunch fresh basil leaves,
    finely chopped
½ pound green beans, trimmed and
    blanched
⅓ cup capers

1 small rustic/country round loaf, cut into
    thick slices and well toasted

Place the tuna steaks in a shallow dish
or bowl, season with salt and pepper to
taste, and drizzle generously with oil. Toss
with all the citrus zest and let sit 30 minutes at room temperature or up to 6 hours
refrigerated.

Make the dressing by whisking together
all the ingredients in a small bowl.

Toss the salad ingredients together in a
mixing bowl.

Heat a skillet over high heat for couple of
minutes. Shake the excess marinade from
the tuna steaks and sear the tuna until
nicely browned on both sides but still rare
in the middle, about 4 minutes per side.

Toss the salad with the dressing.

Place a slice of toasted bread on a dinner
plate and top with the tossed salad. Slice
the tuna steaks thinly and lay over the
salad.

Serves 6

Curried Calamari and Green Bean Stir-Fry Over Coconut-Raisin Rice

I was visiting a friend in Madrid years ago, and this is the late-night
meal I whipped up for us. I'm not sure why I've remembered it all these years;
I guess it's just that tasty. But I figured I'd better get it in
writing before any more time elapses.

For the Rice

1½ cups water
½ cup coconut milk
¼ cup raisins
½ teaspoon salt
1 cup basmati or jasmine rice

For the Calamari

¼ cup pine nuts
1 pound calamari, cleaned and sliced into
    ½-inch slices
3 tablespoons vegetable oil
1 tablespoon curry powder
1 teaspoon sugar
½ teaspoon salt
3 garlic cloves , thinly sliced
½ pound green beans, ends trimmed and
    rinsed
2 tablespoons chopped fresh parsley

Preheat the oven to 350°F.

Make the rice by combining the water,
coconut milk, raisins, and salt in a
saucepan. Bring mixture to a simmer,
add the rice, reduce the heat to low, cover
the pot, and cook 20 minutes.

Spread the pine nuts out on a baking sheet
and bake for about 7 minutes, until toasted
and golden brown.

In a bowl, toss the sliced calamari with
1 tablespoon oil, the curry, sugar, and
salt.

Heat the remaining oil in a large skillet
over high heat just until the oil starts to
smoke. Add the seasoned calamari and
stir-fry for a minute or so. Then add the
garlic and green beans and stir-fry a
couple of minutes longer until the green
beans have softened slightly but are still
bright green.

Remove from the heat, toss with the
parsley, and serve over the rice.

Serves 4

Coconut-Ginger Tilapia Packages With Red Potatoes and Snow Peas

The technique of cooking in an aluminum or parchment package is
called *en papillote*, and it's one of the best ways to cook tender fish because
it gently steams the fish without losing any of the tasty cooking juices. I've made
this meal even easier by including the starch and veggie in the package.
If you're going to be serving this to guests, I'd make an effort to get
parchment paper instead of aluminum foil because it looks much nicer.

4 tilapia fillets

Salt and freshly ground black pepper

1 shallot, finely chopped

1 (1-inch) piece fresh ginger, peeled and
    grated

Zest of 1 lemon

1 cup coconut milk

4 small red potatoes, quartered and sliced
    into ¼-inch pieces

½ pound snow peas

Preheat the oven to 350°F.

Lay the fillets in large double layers of
parchment paper or aluminum foil. Season
to taste with salt and pepper. Divide
the remaining ingredients equally over the
fillets. Roll up the packets tightly, place on
a baking sheet, and bake 25 minutes. Serve
directly in the packets.

Serves 4

Chili Grilled Salmon
With Cucumber-Mango Salsa
and Chipotle Rice

I got tired of pairing salmon with dill, so I came up with this. It's a definite
south-of-the-border twist on things. The cucumber-mango salsa acts
as a cooling agent as well as a sweet foil to the savory fish and rice.

For the Fish

1 pound fresh salmon fillet, skin removed
    and cut into 4 equal pieces
Salt and freshly ground black pepper
3 tablespoons vegetable oil
2 tablespoons chili powder
2 teaspoons dried oregano

For the Cucumber-Mango Salsa

2 ripe but firm mangoes, flesh removed and
    finely diced
1/2 English (hothouse) cucumber, finely diced
Juice of 1 lime
Juice of 1 orange
1 small red onion, finely chopped
1 small bunch fresh mint leaves, finely
    chopped
1/2 teaspoon salt
10 grinds fresh black pepper

For the Rice

2 chipotles packed in adobo, finely chopped,
    with their sauce
1 cup white rice, freshly cooked
1/4 cup packed finely chopped cilantro leaves

Season the fish lightly with salt and pepper to taste. Rub all over with the vegetable oil. Mix the chili powder and oregano together in a small bowl until evenly combined. Rub all over the fish to coat the fish evenly. Let stand, covered, at room temperature for 30 minutes or up to 6 hours in the refrigerator.

Toss all the salsa ingredients together in a mixing bowl.

Finely chop the chipotles, then mix together with the hot cooked rice and the cilantro leaves.

Heat a skillet over high heat. Cook the salmon 4 to 5 minutes per side, until crispy on both sides and cooked until medium or medium rare.

Accompany the salmon with the salsa and rice.

Serves 4

118

Belgian-Style Mussels
With French Fries

I first got a taste of these when I traveled to France as a junior in high school. I was staying with a guest family near the Belgian border and they took me to a beach town one weekend day. I have such a distinct memory of eating mussels and fries (*moules frites*), looking out onto the expansive beach, and smelling the salt water. If you want to have the real Belgian experience, eat the fries dipped in mayonnaise!

For the Mussels

3 tablespoons unsalted butter
4 large garlic cloves, finely chopped
12 ounces pilsner or light ale
2 pounds mussels
2 tablespoons chopped parsley

For the Fries

4 cups vegetable oil, for frying
2 to 3 large Idaho potatoes, about 1 pound
Salt

In a large pot, heat the butter over medium heat. Add the chopped garlic and sauté about 1 minute, but do not brown. Add the beer, then raise the heat to high and bring to a simmer. Add the mussels and cover the pot snugly with a lid. Cook about 7 minutes, until all the mussels have opened. Remove from the heat; discard any unopened mussels. Garnish with parsley and serve.

Heat the vegetable oil over medium-high heat in a heavy pot for about 5 minutes (the temperature should reach around 375°F.).

Slice the potatoes lengthwise into $1/2$-inch slabs, then slice the slabs into thick matchsticks. Cook the fries in batches, about 5 minutes per batch, until well browned and crispy. Lay the finished fries on a plate lined with a double layer of paper towels to absorb any excess oil. Sprinkle generously with salt and serve alongside the mussels.

Serves 4

Pasta

Pasta is one of those rare ingredients that is a gift to the hungry, the poor, and the food snobs of the world alike. A good pasta dish is appreciated by all and a pleasure to make. There's a simple poetry to making pasta, and I am constantly amazed at just how satisfying and rewarding a good bowl of pasta can be. There is no end to what kind of dish pasta can become. It can be a light vegetarian dish or a hearty ragout. Textures can range from thin and soupy to thick and creamy, and pasta is completely neutral, so all flavor combinations work. And even the good stuff is cheap. The good stuff means primarily brands imported from Italy like De Cecco and smaller artisanal producers. You've got to give it to the Italians: When it comes to pasta, they know what they're doing. Good Italian pasta has a starchiness and a body that is pretty much impossible to come by in mass-produced domestic brands. I don't want to sound like a snob, though, because even the lesser pasta still does the job. But for an extra buck, it's worth getting the better-quality pasta. With the exception of a few varieties of pasta, such as gnocchi and ravioli, I generally prefer dried pasta over fresh. That's because I love my pasta al dente, and it's difficult to get that stiffness out of fresh pasta. Fresh pasta is so easily overcooked, and overcooked fresh pasta turns to mush, which is just a bad scene. You can also get dried pastas in many more varieties than fresh pasta, and playing around with the textures and look of all those different shapes is fun. And did I mention that dried pasta is much cheaper than fresh?

Individual Lasagnes

This is a fun family meal. It's not only fun to eat but also fun to make. I had a few kid friends on the show once, and this is what I cooked with them because they're such a blast to make. The easiest thing to do is make these in little mini foil dishes, but if you can find some nice small earthenware dishes, it could actually be quite elegant. Start with a nice salad, and you've got all your bases covered.

For the Sauce

1 (28-ounce) can chopped tomatoes
2 garlic cloves, pressed
2 teaspoons dried oregano
2 teaspoons sugar
Few pinches salt
Few dashes red chili flakes
10 grinds fresh black pepper
1 small bunch fresh parsley, leaves
    coarsely chopped

For the Ricotta

2 cups ricotta
Few pinches salt
About 20 grinds black pepper

For the Veggies

$1/3$ cup olive oil
2 teaspoons salt
1 large zucchini, sliced into $1/8$-inch-thick
    rounds
1 large summer squash, sliced into
    $1/8$-inch-thick rounds
1 small eggplant, sliced into $1/8$-inch-thick
    rounds

1 package uncooked no-boil lasagna noodles
8 ounces mozzarella, shredded

Combine the sauce ingredients in a mixing bowl. Stir well and let sit 30 minutes at room temperature.

In a bowl, mix the ricotta together with the salt and pepper until evenly distributed.

Preheat a grill pan over high heat. Whisk the olive oil and salt to taste together in a bowl. Rub the veggie pieces all over with the olive oil mixture and grill until soft and browned on both sides, about 3 to 4 minutes per side.

Preheat the oven to 375°F.

To assemble the lasagnes: Line the bottom of each of the mini foil baking dishes with a couple of spoonfuls of sauce. Lay a single layer of raw lasagna noodles over that. Next scatter a mixture of the veggies over the top, then an even layer of ricotta. Repeat once more and top it all off with a layer of sauce and plenty of mozzarella.

Place the lasagnes on a baking sheet to catch any dripping cheese. Bake for about 35 minutes, or until bubbly and well browned on top.

Serves 6–8

Spicy Portobello and Asparagus Fettuccine

This is a fantastic vegetarian pasta because the meaty mushrooms are very satisfying. I like to spice up the sauce with red chili flakes, but you can leave those out. Presentation's a cinch. Just throw some shaved Parm on top, and you've got a beautiful rustic dish.

1 pound fettuccine

Extra-virgin olive oil

2 large portobello mushrooms, stems removed, peeled, and sliced about ½ inch thick

Salt

4 garlic cloves, thinly sliced

About 10 dashes red chili flakes (optional)

1 bunch asparagus, bottom quarter trimmed, cut into 2-inch pieces

Parmesan, grana padano, or pecorino Romano cheese for shaving

In a large pot, cook the fettuccine in boiling salted water until al dente. Drain and toss with olive oil to keep the pasta from sticking together.

Heat ¼ cup olive oil in a large skillet over high heat. Toss in the mushrooms, season with salt, and sauté over high heat, browning evenly. Remove the mushrooms from the oil and set aside. Reduce the heat to medium and add the garlic and chili flakes, if using. Cook garlic just a minute or so without browning it. Add the asparagus pieces and cook until they are bright green and slightly softened. Add the mushrooms back to the pan and toss together with the asparagus. Season to taste with salt and toss with the pasta until heated through. Transfer to serving plates and top with the shaved cheese.

Serves 6

Penne With Butternut Squash, Fresh Chorizo, and Thyme

This is rich in all the best senses of the word. Make sure you remove the sausage meat from its casing before you chop it up.

1 pound penne rigate

Salt

Extra-virgin olive oil

¾ pound fresh chorizo, casing removed and meat chopped

½ pound peeled butternut squash, cut into ¾-inch cubes

4 garlic cloves, finely chopped

About 10 thyme sprigs

15 grinds fresh black pepper

In a large pot, cook the penne in boiling salted water until al dente. Drain and toss with olive oil to keep the pasta from sticking together.

Heat 2 tablespoons of olive oil in a large nonstick skillet over high heat. Brown the chopped sausage meat, then transfer to a plate but leave the fat in the pan. Add 2 tablespoons more oil to the pan.
Add the squash and cook 5 minutes, not stirring too often, so the squash gets some color. Reduce the heat to medium-low, add the garlic, thyme, black pepper, and browned sausage, and cook 7 to 10 minutes, tossing often, until the squash is fork-tender but not falling apart. Toss with the pasta and garnish with a thyme sprig or two from the pan.

Serves 6

Spaghetti With Mint and Parsley Pesto

I call this a pesto sauce, but it doesn't have nuts in it, so it's not pesto in the strictest sense. I wanted to keep this spaghetti as light and fresh as possible, so I left them out. The herbaceous, vibrant color and flavor of the sauce is astonishing.

For the Pesto

2 large bunches mint
2 large bunches parsley
¾ cup extra-virgin olive oil
Juice of 1 lemon
4 garlic cloves
½ cup grated Parmesan, pecorino, or
    grana padano cheese
1 teaspoon salt

1 pound spaghetti

Blend the pesto ingredients together in a blender or food processor.

In a large pot, cook the spaghetti until al dente and toss with the pesto.

Serves 6

{ Pesto is best made as close to the time of serving as possible because it will slowly lose its bright green color. If you do make it ahead of time, put it in an airtight container and store in the fridge.

Creamy Shrimp Fettuccine

You don't want to throw too much at shrimp. A little garlic, white wine, and cream, and that's it. When the shrimp changes all over to a bright orange color, they're done. Don't overcook them.

1 pound fettuccine
Extra-virgin olive oil
1½ cups heavy cream
½ cup white wine
5 garlic cloves, thinly sliced
20 grinds fresh black pepper
1 pound peeled deveined shrimp
2 tablespoons finely chopped fresh parsley

Cook the fettuccine in a large pot of boiling, salted water until al dente, about 7 minutes. Toss the pasta with some oil to keep it from sticking while you make the sauce.

Combine the cream, wine, garlic, and black pepper in a large skillet and bring to a simmer over high heat. Reduce the heat to medium and simmer 7 to 10 minutes, until the mixture thickens. Add the shrimp and cook, 4 to 5 minutes. Toss the sauce with the pasta and the chopped parsley.

Serves 6

Buy frozen shrimp rather than fresh. They're cheaper frozen in the bag and it's exactly what your supermarket fish counter is selling as "fresh." The quickest way to defrost shrimp is to put them in a large bowl and run cool water over them for a few minutes, then strain them dry.

Twisted Pasta With Browned Butter, Sage, and Walnuts

Browned butter and sage is one of those classic combinations that seems almost too good to be true. There are two tricks to making this dish out of this world: not burning the butter and not cooking the pasta past al dente. If you can manage these two things, you're in for a real treat.

About ½ cup walnut halves

1 pound twisted pasta such as campanelle, caserecci, or cavatelli

2 sticks unsalted butter

2 bunches sage leaves, large stems plucked

Preheat the oven to 350°F.

Lay walnuts out on a baking sheet and bake about 7 minutes, until toasted and fragrant.

Cook the pasta in a large pot of boiling salted water until al dente.

In a skillet, melt the butter over medium heat. Continue to heat the butter until it turns light brown. Add the sage leaves to the butter and cook until crisped and the butter has turned another shade darker, but be sure to remove from the heat before it burns.

Toss the butter and sage gently with the pasta, being careful not to break the sage leaves up too much. Divide the pasta among serving bowls and top with the crushed toasted walnuts.

Serves 6

Farfalle With Garlic, Peas, and Bacon

This is another pasta that seems too simple and too good to be true. But true it is. Brown your bacon well to get the richest flavor possible.

1 pound farfalle
Extra-virgin olive oil
½ pound bacon, finely chopped
4 garlic cloves, thinly sliced
½ pound frozen peas
1 small bunch parsley, finely chopped
Salt and freshly ground black pepper
Freshly grated Parmesan cheese

Cook the farfalle in a large pot of boiling salted water until al dente, then toss with some olive oil to keep the pasta from sticking.

Brown the bacon in a large skillet over high heat. Pour off some of the rendered fat, then add the garlic and and cook a minute or so. Then add the peas and cook until heated through but still bright green. Toss with the pasta until the noodles are hot, then stir in the chopped parsley and season to taste with salt and pepper.

Spoon onto plates and finish with grated Parmesan cheese.

Serves 6

Easy Mushroom Risotto

Traditional risotto is quite a laborious process because you have to stand over the rice and stir it constantly as it absorbs liquid, which you add little by little. This careful ritual has its payoff, but this much easier version certainly has its charms in that you don't have to do any of the above. And it's darn tasty, too. You can either serve this as a meal in itself or as a side for a hearty, flavorful piece of meat.

1 ounce dried mushrooms such as shiitake
   or porcini
1 cup boiling water
3 tablespoons olive oil
1 shallot, minced
1 cup arborio rice
1½ cups reduced-sodium chicken stock
½ cup dry white wine
Few pinches salt
2 tablespoons unsalted butter
½ cup grated Parmesan or Pecorino
   Romano cheese
2 tablespoons chopped fresh parsley

Place the mushrooms in a bowl, pour the boiling water over them, cover, and let sit 10 minutes.

Heat the oil in a large saucepan over medium heat. Add the shallot and sweat until it starts to turn translucent in color, just a couple of minutes. Add the rice, stirring all the grains to coat them with oil. Cook a minute or so. Add the stock and wine. Remove the mushrooms from their liquid, reserving the liquid, and chop them roughly. Add the mushrooms with their liquid to the mixture. Add the salt and raise the heat to medium-high. Bring to a simmer. Stir well, reduce the heat to low, cover, and cook 20 minutes, stirring once more after 10 minutes. Remove from the heat. Stir in the butter, cheese, and parsley.

Serves 4–6

Baked Ricotta and
Spinach Rigatoni

This is a one-pot, one-dish meal. If you can get your hands on smoked mozzarella
instead of the regular stuff, you'll take the flavor to the next level.

1 pound rigatoni

Extra-virgin olive oil

4 tablespoons (½ stick) unsalted butter

1 large shallot, minced

2 garlic cloves, pressed

¼ cup all-purpose flour

½ cup white wine

2 cups milk

½ teaspoon ground nutmeg

Salt and freshly ground black pepper

2 (10-ounce) packages frozen chopped
   spinach, thawed and excess water
   strained

2 cups ricotta cheese

2 eggs, lightly beaten

½ pound mozzarella (preferably smoked),
   grated

Preheat the oven to 350°F.

Cook the pasta in a large pot of boiling
salted water for 5 minutes. Drain and toss
with a drizzle of olive oil to keep the pasta
from sticking together.

Melt the butter in a large saucepan over
medium heat. When the butter starts to
bubble, add the shallot and garlic and
sweat a few minutes until softened and
mellowed in pungency. Add the flour and
stir until a smooth paste forms. Gradually
whisk in the wine and milk. Bring the mixture to a simmer, whisking all the while.
Cook until thickened, about 5 minutes.
Season with the nutmeg and salt and
pepper to taste.

Transfer the béchamel sauce to a large
mixing bowl and combine with the spinach,
ricotta, and eggs. Mix in the pasta and
transfer to a baking dish just large
enough to hold the mixture. Top with
the grated mozzarella, cover loosely with
aluminum foil, and bake 40 minutes.
Remove the foil and bake 20 minutes
longer, until the cheese has lightly
browned on top, the center is no longer
runny, and the sides are bubbly.

Serves 8

Creamy Lemon Almond Linguine

This pasta dish is about as simply elegant as it gets. Its rich, creamy, silky texture makes it indulgent, too. Cooking the sauce over steam as opposed to direct heat is important, so as not to scramble the egg yolks. The process of cooking over the boiling water thickens the sauce and eliminates any worries about unwanted bacteria. I like to buy eggy pasta to highlight the yolky goodness of the sauce.

1 pound linguine
Extra-virgin olive oil
5 egg yolks
¾ cup heavy cream
1 shallot, minced
Zest of 1 lemon and juice of ½ lemon, a pinch of zest reserved for garnish
Salt
½ cup ground whole almonds, a couple pinches reserved for garnish

In a large pot of boiling salted water, cook the linguine until al dente and toss with oil to keep it from sticking.

Combine the egg yolks, heavy cream, shallot, lemon zest, lemon juice, and a couple of pinches of salt in a heatproof bowl. Place over a pot of boiling water and whisk regularly until the mixture thickens into a pale yellow, silky consistency.

Remove from the heat, stir in the almonds, and toss with the linguine.

Garnish with more lemon zest and ground almonds.

Serves 6

Apricot-Dijon Roasted Pork Chops
With Kale and Mushroom
Wild Rice, page 143

Meat

believe that we, as humans, are programmed to eat and savor meat. So even before you go into the spice cabinet to think about your seasonings, you're already off to a good start if you have a hunk of meat on your counter. You have to work pretty darn hard to make a piece of meat completely unappetizing.

I've focused on cuts of meat that are more affordable than top-shelf cuts like rib eye and filet mignon because you don't really need a recipe for those cuts. The best way to cook those cuts is to salt and pepper them and cook them quickly in a hot pan or on the grill. But more than that, good steaks can be prohibitively expensive and the cheaper cuts can be just as tasty; they simply require a little more attention. Some tougher cuts, such as shoulder and roasting cuts, can be made wonderfully succulent and tender by cooking them on low heat for a long time. Other cuts, such as skirt and flank steak, shouldn't be cooked past medium.

Apricot-Dijon Roasted Pork Chops With Kale and Mushroom Wild Rice

Wild rice is expensive, but it's a shame not to use it. So I simply cut down
on the amount of wild rice I use by mixing it half and half with regular
white rice. I like this almost better anyhow, because it provides a
light base for the heavier, chewier wild rice.

For the Pork Chops

4 bone-in pork chops, about ⅓ pound each
Salt and freshly ground black pepper
½ cup apricot marmalade
2 teaspoons Dijon mustard
1 teaspoon Worcestershire sauce
Leaves from about 10 fresh thyme sprigs

For the Wild Rice

3 tablespoons olive oil
1 (12-ounce) package button mushrooms,
    stems removed and chopped in ½-inch
    pieces
Salt and freshly ground black pepper
1 medium onion, cut into medium dice
1 pound bunch of kale, bottom stems and
    spines removed, leaves roughly chopped
1 cup short-grain white rice, cooked
1 cup wild rice, cooked

Preheat the oven to 400°F.

Place the pork chops on a baking sheet.
Salt and pepper them on both sides.

Stir the marmalade, mustard, Worcestershire, and thyme in a bowl until thoroughly
combined. Slather the mixture all over the
pork chops until entirely and evenly
coated.

Roast about 20 minutes, until browned and
cooked through but still juicy and tender.

Make the wild rice: Heat the oil in a
saucepan over high heat for a couple of
minutes to get it really hot. Add the mushrooms and season generously with salt
and pepper to taste. Sauté until the
mushrooms give off their water, the water
evaporates, and the mushrooms start to
brown. Add the onion and sauté until
softened and translucent. Add the kale
and cover tightly with a lid so that the
greens wilt. Once the greens have wilted
slightly, toss with the mushrooms and
onions and sauté until the kale becomes
tender but still bright green. Add more oil
if the mixture is dry. Add the rices and stir
all the ingredients together. Season with
salt and pepper to taste.

Serves 4

Beer-Braised Barbecued Pork Butt
Over Cheesy Grits

I fell in love with pulled pork on a spring break road trip down to Florida. We stopped off of I-95 in Georgia at a wooden hut that only does barbecue, and that's where I had my first pulled pork sandwich. They cook their pork up to eighteen hours, so this version can't thoroughly compete, but when you add the homemade barbecue sauce it's really very good. The creamy grits are classic and just right.

For the Pork

3 tablespoons vegetable oil

2 tablespoons salt

1 tablespoon sugar

About 50 grinds black pepper

2 tablespoons chili powder

1 tablespoon garlic powder

2 teaspoons ground coriander

2 teaspoons ground mustard seed

1 pork butt, about 5-6 pounds

12 ounces good ale or dark beer, such as
    Bass

5 garlic cloves, thinly sliced

½ cup ketchup

2 tablespoons whole grain Dijon mustard

3 tablespoons Worcestershire sauce

⅓ cup dark brown sugar

For the Grits

3 cups whole milk

1 teaspoon salt

1 cup instant grits

1 cup grated sharp white Cheddar cheese

Combine the oil, salt, sugar, pepper, chili powder, garlic powder, coriander, and mustard seed in a bowl and mix well. Rub all over the pork butt. Wrap in plastic and refrigerate for at least 2 hours but preferably overnight.

Preheat the oven to 500°F. Unwrap the pork and place in a roasting pan with sides just a couple of inches high. If your pan is too high, the meat won't brown well. Cook 45 minutes, until dark browned and blackening in places. Remove from the oven. Lower the oven to 300°F. Pour the beer over the top and add the sliced garlic to the beer around the pork. Cover tightly with heavy-duty aluminum foil or twice with regular foil. Poke about 10 holes all over the top of the foil. Cook the pork butt 2½ hours longer, until it is so tender that it comes away very easily from the center bone. Cook longer if necessary.

Place the meat on a plate and pour the pan juice (there will be plenty) into a saucepan. To the pan juices add the ketchup, mustard, Worcestershire, and brown sugar. Stir together and bring to a boil. Simmer until thick and reduced by half, about 20 minutes.

While the sauce is boiling down, pull apart the pork with two forks. Pour the sauce over the pulled pork and work through until fully absorbed.

Make the grits: Scald the milk with the salt in a saucepan over medium heat until little bubbles appear around the outside. Slowly whisk in the grits and continue whisking until the mixture barely simmers. Cook, whisking often, until very thick, about 5 to 6 minutes. Remove from the heat and stir in the cheese until melted and smooth.

Serve the savory pulled pork over the hot grits.

Serves 8

Braised Hoisin Short Ribs With Mashed Yukons and Sesame Snow Peas

When beef ribs are braised right, they become one of the most succulent, decadent pieces of meat out there. They are this way because of their incredible fat content. Don't be scared of it, embrace it. It's a special dish. To offset the fat, you need something sweet and tangy, which provides the perfect opening for hoisin sauce. Hoisin also has a rich soy flavor that enhances the richness of the ribs. Only simple fare should accompany ribs, but adding a little toasted sesame to the snow peas completes the circle of Asian flavors.

For the Ribs

3 pounds beef short ribs, about 10 ribs
Salt and freshly ground black pepper
3 tablespoons vegetable oil
10 to 12 garlic cloves, smashed
1 (2-inch) piece fresh ginger, peeled and sliced into ¼-inch slices
12 ounces good ale
3 tablespoons rice wine vinegar
1 cup hoisin sauce

For the Mashed Yukons

About 2 pounds Yukon gold potatoes, peeled
4 tablespoons (½ stick) unsalted butter, melted
2 large shallots, minced
½ cup heavy cream
Salt and freshly ground black pepper

For the Sesame Snow Peas

1 pound snow peas
3 tablespoons vegetable oil
1 tablespoon dark sesame oil
Salt
1 tablespoon sesame seeds, toasted

Preheat the oven to 325°F.

Season the ribs generously with salt and pepper to taste. Heat the vegetable oil in a large heavy ovenproof pot with a lid (such as a Dutch oven) over high heat. Brown the ribs on all sides, in batches if necessary. Remove the ribs and pour off all but a couple of tablespoons of the rendered fat.

Return the pot to the stove, lower the heat to medium, and sauté the garlic and ginger for about 3 minutes. Add the ribs back to the pot. Add the ale and vinegar. Stir, cover, and move to the oven. Bake 2 hours.

continued

146

Braised Hoisin Short Ribs With Mashed Yukons and Sesame Snow Peas (continued)

Boil the potatoes until fork-tender. Drain the potatoes, return them to the pot, and mash with a hand masher.

Heat the butter in a saucepan over medium heat until it starts to bubble. Add the shallots and sauté until softened and slightly translucent. Add the cream and heat until steaming.

Add the hot liquid to the potatoes and mash further until smooth. Season to taste with salt and pepper.

Remove the ribs from the oven. Pour the hoisin sauce over the ribs, return to the oven, uncovered, and cook 20 to 30 minutes longer, until the ribs are falling-off-the-bone tender with a moist, glossy glaze finish to them.

Rinse the peas and trim off the ends. In a large saucepan, add the oils and heat over medium-high heat. Add the snow peas and sauté until bright green, about 2 to 3 minutes. Season with salt, sprinkle with a couple teaspoons of the seeds, and toss.

Serve the ribs over the potatoes, top with a good drizzling of the cooking juices, and surround with the snow peas. Garnish with the remaining sesame seeds.

Serves about 6

Dad's Sweet-and-Sour Stuffed Red Cabbage *(continued)*

Preheat the oven to 350°F. Bring a large pot of salted water to a boil.

Cut off the bottom quarter of the cabbage. Fully remove the inner core of the cabbage with the tip of your chef's knife, essentially hollowing out a large portion of the cabbage.

Drop the cored cabbage into the boiling water and cook 40 minutes. Remove and let sit until cool enough to touch.

While the cabbage is boiling, make the stuffing by mixing together the beef, onion, garlic, salt, pepper, Worcestershire sauce, and rice in a mixing bowl.

Pull apart the leaves of the cabbage one by one until you reach leaves that are too small to use as wrapping leaves. Shred the smaller leaves and reserve for the sauce.

Make the sauce: Heat the oil in a large pot over medium-high heat. Sweat the onion until soft and translucent, about 5 minutes. Add the shredded inner part of the cabbage, the tomatoes, sugar, vinegar, and raisins. Stir to combine. Simmer 10 minutes, then season with salt to taste.

Form a small ball of the stuffing mixture in the palm of your hand. Wrap in a softened cabbage leaf and place in a large skillet or baking dish. Form as many of these "packages" as possible. Pour the sauce over the top of the stuffed cabbages and bake, uncovered, for 45 minutes.

Serves 8

Braised Lamb Shoulder Chops With Kale and Cannellini Beans

Shoulder lamb chops are one of the cheapest cuts from the lamb, but when you cook them this way, they are incredibly tender and delicious. It couldn't be easier either: Everything goes into a big pot and you let it cook until the meat is falling off the bone and the beans have absorbed the rich lamb juices and flavors.

3 tablespoons extra-virgin olive oil

4 shoulder lamb chops, about $\frac{1}{3}$ pound each

1 large onion, chopped

8 garlic cloves, thinly sliced

1 tablespoon all-purpose flour

2 cups beef or lamb stock

1 cup canned crushed tomatoes

2 (15-ounce) cans cannellini beans, rinsed and strained

2 large rosemary sprigs

$\frac{1}{2}$ pound kale, washed, stems and ribs removed, and roughly chopped

Salt and freshly ground black pepper

Preheat the oven to 300°F.

Heat a large heavy ovenproof pot with a lid (such as a Dutch oven) over high heat for a couple of minutes. Add the oil. Season the lamb chops generously with salt and pepper. Brown the lamb chops on both sides. Remove the lamb chops from the pot. Add the onion and garlic and cook until the onion starts to turn translucent. Add the flour and stir until incorporated. Stir in the remaining ingredients (don't worry about the kale so much; it won't want to be mixed in but it will wilt in as the dish cooks), add lamb back to the pot, and bring to a simmer, then cover snugly with a lid, and transfer to the oven. Cook $1\frac{3}{4}$ hours until the lamb falls apart easily with the slightest prodding from a fork.

Serves 4

Lamb Tagine Over Moroccan-Style Couscous

A tagine is actually the cooking vessel traditionally used to make this North African braised dish. The tagine looks like a cone and does wonders to make super tender, juicy stewed meats. But you don't need a tagine to make this dish; a regular ovenproof pot will do fine.

For the Tagine

1 (4- to 5-pound) boneless leg of lamb, silver skin and sinews cut away, and cut into 2-inch cubes

Salt and freshly ground black pepper

¼ cup vegetable oil

1 medium onion, cut into medium dice

10 garlic cloves, smashed

4 rosemary sprigs

2 whole cinnamon sticks

1 good pinch ground cloves (optional)

1 pound sweet potatoes, peeled and cut into 1- to 2-inch cubes

½ pound pitted prunes

1 navel orange, cut into 2-inch pieces

2 bottles good pale ale

For the Couscous

3 tablespoons vegetable oil

1 medium onion, finely chopped

3 garlic cloves, pressed

1 teaspoon ground cinnamon

2 medium zucchini (about ½ pound), cut in half lengthwise and then into ¼-inch slices

1 (19-ounce) can chickpeas, drained

½ cup raisins, packed

1 cup canned crushed tomatoes

3 cups couscous, cooked

Salt

Preheat the oven to 325°F.

Season the lamb with salt and pepper to taste. Heat the oil in a tagine or Dutch oven over high heat and brown lamb in batches. Set aside the browned lamb and sauté the onion and garlic for a couple of minutes. Add the lamb back to the pot and then add the remaining ingredients. Cover and cook for 3 hours.

About ½ hour before the tagine is ready, make the couscous: Heat the vegetable oil in a large skillet over medium heat. Add the onion and garlic and sauté until the onion starts to soften. Add the cinnamon and stir to combine. Add the zucchini and sauté until the zucchini starts to soften but is still bright green. Add the chickpeas, raisins, and tomatoes, bring to a simmer, and cook 5 minutes, until thickened and no longer runny. Fluff the couscous with a fork, then add the vegetable mixture to the couscous and mix in thoroughly. Season with salt to taste.

Serves 6–8

159

Pan-Grilled Skirt Steak With Smoky Cowboy Beans and Minted Chimichurri Sauce

Skirt steak is often overlooked in the supermarket, but it is one of my all-time favorite cuts of beef. It is very rich, but not overwhelmingly so because the fat is evenly distributed throughout. For my money, the best way to cook skirt steak is to flash-fry it or grill it so you don't cook it past medium rare. I always associate skirt steak with chili flavor, so my favorite way to season it is with some good, spicy chili powder. Beans are a natural fit and the chimichurri sauce, a classic South American condiment, offers freshness from the herbs and brightness from the acid.

For Steak

2 medium skirt steaks
Salt and freshly ground black pepper
¼ cup olive or vegetable oil
3 tablespoons chili powder
2 tablespoons dried oregano
4 garlic cloves, minced or pressed

For Chimichurri Sauce

1 bunch finely chopped parsley leaves
1 bunch finely chopped cilantro leaves
1 bunch finely chopped mint leaves
½ cup olive oil
¼ cup red wine vinegar
Juice of 1 lemon
2 garlic cloves, pressed
½ teaspoon salt

For Beans

½ pound sliced bacon, finely chopped
1 large red onion, cut into medium dice
6 garlic cloves, finely chopped
26 ounces chopped tomatoes
1 quart reduced-sodium beef or chicken
   stock
Few fresh thyme sprigs
2 (15-ounce) cans kidney beans, rinsed
1 (15-ounce) can black beans, rinsed
1 (15-ounce) can pinto beans, rinsed
1 teaspoon salt
About 40 grinds pepper
3 tablespoons dark brown sugar
3 teaspoons Worcestershire Sauce

Place the skirt steaks in a large bowl or baking dish, season both sides with salt and pepper to taste, then add the oil, chili powder, oregano, and garlic. Rub all over until the steaks are evenly coated. Let sit 30 minutes at room temperature and up to a few hours in the refrigerator.

Make the chimichurri sauce: Combine all the ingredients in a bowl and mix thoroughly. The sauce can be made up to 12 hours in advance and stored in the refrigerator in a tightly sealed container.

Make the beans: Sauté the bacon in a large, heavy-bottomed pot over medium-high heat until brown and the fat has rendered. Add the onion and garlic and sauté until the onion starts to turn translucent.

Add the remaining ingredients and bring the mixture to a simmer. Reduce the heat to medium-low and simmer for 1 hour.

Cook the steak: Heat a grill pan over high heat for 5 minutes. Grill the steak 4 minutes on each side for medium and 5 minutes on each side for medium well.

Spoon a portion of beans onto each plate. Slice the skirt steak and serve over the top of the beans. Drizzle chimichurri sauce around the steak and beans.

Serves 6

Prune- and Walnut-Stuffed Pork Roast With Creamy Cheddar Cauliflower

Stuffing a pork loin achieves a few goals. Cutting up the meat before cooking tenderizes it, and stuffing it with tasty ingredients adds flavor from the inside and makes for a winning presentation.

For the Roast

1 medium pork loin roast, about 2 pounds
⅓ cup extra-virgin olive oil
1 medium onion, finely diced
½ pound pitted dried plums (prunes), roughly chopped
2 Macintosh apples, peeled, cored, and roughly chopped
¼ pound walnut pieces, roughly chopped (about 1 cup)
2 tablespoons finely chopped fresh rosemary leaves
Juice and zest of ½ lemon

For the Cheddar Cauliflower

2 heads cauliflower, about 1½ pounds each
4 tablespoons (½ stick) unsalted butter
⅓ cup all-purpose flour
2 cups milk
½ cup white wine
1 teaspoon salt
25 grinds fresh black pepper
Dash ground nutmeg (optional)
1 cup grated sharp white Cheddar cheese

Preheat the oven to 350°F.

Cut into the pork roast horizontally to flay it open and create a flat, even layer of meat. Combine the remaining ingredients in a mixing bowl and toss well.

continued

Prune- and Walnut-Stuffed Pork Roast
With Creamy Cheddar Cauliflower *(continued)*

Spread some of the mixture over the open surface of the flayed pork loin. Fold up as tightly as possible and place in a large baking pan or dish, opening-side down. Spread the rest of the filling around and over the roast.

Cover loosely with aluminum foil and bake 1½ hours.

Break apart the rinsed, dried cauliflower into florets. Put in a baking pan that holds the cauliflower florets snugly but still has a couple of inches of room on the top.

In a large saucepan, melt the butter over medium heat. Add the flour to the melted butter and whisk together until smooth.

Cook a minute or two, then gradually add the milk, constantly whisking to make sure the mixture stays smooth and creamy. Add the wine, salt, pepper, and nutmeg. Continue to cook, still constantly whisking, until thickened, about 4 to 5 minutes. Whisk in the Cheddar until fully melted. Season to taste with more salt and pepper if needed, then pour the sauce over the cauliflower in an even layer. Cover loosely with aluminum foil and bake until the cauliflower is tender, about 40 minutes. Serve with the sliced pork roast.

Serves 8

Roasted Rosemary and Lemon Pork Tenderloin With Pomegranate Reduction and Gorgonzola Polenta

Pork tenderloin is tender and moist, and has a really nice subtle pork flavor. It is also so inexpensive compared to other cuts of meat of the same quality. Because it's such a mild piece of meat, you don't want to throw really heavy flavors at it—rosemary and lemon are just perfect. The pomegranate adds some needed acidity and pairs beautifully with all the other ingredients. You can find pomegranate juice in small containers now in almost every supermarket and even convenience stores. Since it's become so readily available, I've added it to my list of kitchen staples.

¼ cup olive oil
3 garlic cloves, pressed
Finely grated zest of 1 lemon
2 good pinches salt
About 25 grinds fresh black pepper
2 pork tenderloins, about 1½ pounds each
5 fresh rosemary sprigs, plus a couple more
   for garnish

1 cup 100% pomegranate juice, such as POM

For Polenta
1 quart reduced-sodium chicken stock
1 cup instant polenta
⅓ cup heavy cream
4 to 6 ounces Gorgonzola cheese
Salt and freshly ground black pepper

Preheat the oven to 400°F.

Whisk together the olive oil, garlic, lemon zest, salt, and pepper in a small mixing bowl with a fork.

Place the tenderloins in a large ovenproof skillet. Rub the oil combination all over the tenderloins. Toss with the rosemary sprigs. Prepare up to a day in advance and store in a large resealable bag in the fridge. Bring back to room temperature before roasting.

Roast for 25 to 30 minutes, until cooked through but still moist and tender.

Bring the chicken stock to a simmer in a saucepan, gradually whisk in the polenta, and whisk constantly for 3 to 4 minutes, until the mixture thickens considerably.

continued

Roasted Rosemary and Lemon Pork Tenderloin With Pomegranate Reduction and Gorgonzola Polenta *(continued)*

Add the heavy cream and cheese and cook 2 minutes longer. Season to taste with salt and pepper.

When the tenderloins have finished cooking, remove from the pan and set aside on a cutting board.

Pour off most of the oil from the pan, leaving as many browned bits as possible. Place the pan on the stovetop over medium-high heat. (Be careful of the hot handle!) Add the pomegranate juice and reduce by at least half until slightly thickened.

Slice the tenderloin, serve over the polenta, and top with the reduction. Garnish with small sprigs of fresh rosemary.

Serves 8

Red Wine Pot Roast
With Honey and Thyme

I couldn't create a meat section without a pot roast recipe. This is the ultimate one-pot meal, and so low maintenance. Pot roast is an inexpensive way to get a lot of tasty meat. The honey and thyme add a really nice perfume to the dish. Pot roast refers to the way the meat is cooked, not the cut itself, so there are a few cuts that make for good pot roast. I've listed the most common ones but chuck is the best because of its good, even marbling.

1 (4-pound) chuck roast, rump, top, or
    bottom round if chuck is not available
Salt and freshly ground black pepper
3 tablespoons vegetable oil
3 small onions, cut into medium dice
10 garlic cloves, lightly smashed
1 pound carrots, cut roughly into 1-inch
    pieces
3 ounces tomato paste
2 cups reduced-sodium beef, chicken, or
    vegetable stock
2 cups red wine
2 tablespoons honey
8 fresh thyme sprigs
2 pounds russet potatoes, peeled and cut
    into 1½-inch cubes

Season the roast with salt and pepper to taste.

Heat the oil in a large ovenproof pot, such as a Dutch oven, over high heat for a couple of minutes. Add the meat and brown well on all sides. Remove and set aside on a plate. Lower the heat to medium. Add the onions, garlic, and carrots and cook for 5 minutes, stirring often. Stir in the tomato paste and cook a couple of minutes longer. Add the stock, wine, honey, and thyme, stir, and then add the roast back to the pot. Cover the pot and transfer to the oven. Bake 2½ hours, turning twice. Uncover, add the potatoes to the pot, and bake, uncovered, 45 minutes longer, until both the potatoes and meat are fork-tender.

Serves 6

One Dough, Three Cookies, page 184

Desserts

After a big, satisfying meal, there's not necessarily a need to put out dessert. No one would really go hungry without it, but dessert isn't about necessity; it's about luxury and indulgence. That's why desserts have to be something extraordinary. That doesn't mean fancy—some of my favorite desserts are the simple ones like fruit crumbles and chocolate cake—but it does mean that it needs to be something you couldn't pick up from the supermarket bakery department. To me, it's almost as if I can taste the love in home-baked desserts, probably because it was always people I love who were baking for me, my father and grandmother in particular. I suppose because desserts do have a certain specialness, they can be an expression of love. Of course they don't have to be; sometimes a good dessert is just a good dessert.

I've really gotten into baking over the last couple of years. Being a good baker takes a lot of practice and a lot of frustration if you refuse to follow a recipe, like me. I was actually a terrible baker until I put myself to the task of getting good at it. It took years of repetition and messing up. But now that I can bake, I've got the bug, which is why a lot of my dessert recipes involve baking. One thing I've tried to do is keep baking as streamlined as possible, using as few steps as possible, and using as few utensils and bowls as possible. Baking is a commitment, but it gives back in fulfillment and pride.

And if you can't even stand the thought of baking, I've included a few other recipes that don't even ask you to turn on the oven.

Apple Crumble
With Vanilla Ice Cream

Here's a classic that never gets tired—although, come to think of it, I can't remember seeing one of these on a menu recently. Good, then, that I'm putting it on mine!

For Filling

5 large Golden Delicious apples
    (about 3 pounds)
1 cup granulated sugar
Juice of 1 lemon
1/4 cup brandy
1/2 teaspoon ground cinnamon

For Crumble

About 1 cup chopped walnuts or pecans
1 cup all-purpose flour
1 1/4 cups rolled oats
1/2 cup dark brown sugar
1 teaspoon ground cinnamon
Pinch salt
1 stick cold unsalted butter, cut into small
    pieces

Vanilla ice cream, as an accompaniment

Preheat the oven to 350°F.

Peel, core, and the slice the apples into 1/4-inch slices. Transfer the apples to a large mixing bowl and toss with the granulated sugar, lemon juice, brandy, and cinnamon. Pour into a lightly greased 13 × 9-inch baking dish.

In another large bowl, make a coarse crumb mixture out of the crumble ingredients, using your fingers. Top the apples with this mixture and bake about 45 minutes.

Serve warm with vanilla ice cream.

Serves 8

Challah Bread Pudding With Chocolate, Raisins, and Vanilla Cream

This bread pudding is heavenly and sinful at the same time. I use dense, rich challah bread that sets into a creamy soft custard. But it's the chocolate and raisins layered in between the slices of bread that really make the dish. Of course, some more fresh vanilla cream on top doesn't hurt either.

For the Bread Pudding

1 quart whole milk, warmed
1 stick unsalted butter, melted
1½ cups sugar
6 eggs
1 teaspoon pure vanilla extract
1 challah, cut into 1½-inch slices
1 cup chocolate chips
½ cup raisins

For the Vanilla Cream

2 cups half-and-half
2 teaspoons pure vanilla extract
⅓ cup sugar
6 egg yolks

Preheat the oven to 325°F.

Combine the milk, butter, sugar, eggs, and vanilla in a large mixing bowl. Whisk until incorporated and smooth, but don't over-whisk.

Line a baking dish with two thirds of the challah slices, lining the edges too. Sprinkle with half the chocolate chips and half the raisins. Cover with the remaining challah slices, layering them one on top of the other. Top with the remaining chocolate chips and raisins, making sure the chips and raisins get inside the layers created by the challah slices. Pour the milk mixture over the top of everything.

Wrap the baking dish tightly with aluminum foil. Bake 50 minutes, then remove the foil and cook 15 minutes longer, until set in the middle and lightly browned on top.

While the pudding is baking, make the vanilla cream: Combine the half-and-half, vanilla, and sugar in a large saucepan. Heat over medium heat, whisking regularly, until steaming hot. Place the egg yolks in a large mixing bowl and gradually add the hot half-and-half mixture to the egg yolks, whisking vigorously all the while. When all the half-and-half mixture has been whisked into the egg yolks, return the mixture to the saucepan and heat over medium heat, whisking constantly. Cook until the mixture thickens. Spoon over the pudding and serve.

Serves 10–12

Chocolate Guinness Cupcakes

I love cooking with beer, and that's no exception when it comes to desserts. Of all beers, Guinness is the perfect one for desserts because of its distinct chocolate and coffee notes. Pairing it with actual chocolate is the obvious choice. These cupcakes are light in texture, but heavy in the chocolate department. The white cream cheese icing reminds me of the creamy white head that Guinness is famous for.

1 (12-ounce) bottle Guinness stout
½ cup milk
½ cup vegetable oil
1 tablespoon pure vanilla extract
3 large eggs
¾ cup sour cream
¾ cup unsweetened cocoa, plus more for garnish
2 cups sugar
2½ cups all-purpose flour
1½ teaspooons baking soda

For the Frosting
1 (8-ounce) package cream cheese, softened
⅓ cup heavy cream
1 pound confectioners' sugar

Cocoa powder, for dusting

Preheat the oven to 350°F.

In a large mixing bowl, combine the Guinness, milk, vegetable oil, and vanilla. Beat in the eggs, one at time. Mix in the sour cream.

In a large mixing bowl, whisk together the cocoa, sugar, flour, and baking soda. Gradually mix the dry ingredients into the wet Guinness mixture.

Butter 24 muffin tins and divide the batter among the muffin tins.

Bake 25 minutes, until risen and set in the middle but still soft and tender. Cool before turning out of the tins.

Make the frosting: Beat the cream cheese in a bowl until light and fluffy. Gradually beat in the heavy cream. Slowly mix in the confectioners' sugar.

Top each cupcake with a heap of frosting and dust with cocoa.

Makes 24

Lemon Blueberry Cheesecake With Shortbread Cookie Crust

I love cheesecake. The trick to cheesecake is getting the right balance between the rich, heavy quality of cream cheese and a light fluffy texture. I think I've got it here. I like to taste a little tang from the cream cheese, so I don't oversweeten it, and I go light on the lemon flavor. The lemon flavor is a beautiful thing, though, because it has a palate-cleansing quality that cuts the creamy richness. The blueberry jam pairs perfectly with the lemon and makes the cake look impressive. Because of the water content, you're likely to get some cracks in the cake, but that's okay.

For the crust

10 ounces shortbread cookies, such as Werners or Lorna Doones
½ cup dark brown sugar
½ stick unsalted butter, melted

For the Filling

24 ounces cream cheese, at room temperature
¾ cup sour cream
3 eggs, at room temperature, lightly beaten
1 cup granulated sugar
1 teaspoon pure vanilla extract
Grated zest of 1 small lemon
3 tablespoons good blueberry jam, thinned with a couple of teaspoons warm water if necessary

Preheat the oven to 325°F.

Place the cookies in a food processor or blender and process until you get fine crumbs. Place the crumbs in a 12-inch pie plate. Stir in the brown sugar with a fork until evenly distributed. Add the melted butter and use your fingers to work the butter into the crumbs. When the butter has been evenly worked into the crumbs, mound the crumbs into a tight heap in the middle of the pie plate and press down and up the sides to make an even crust. Press the sides so they're not too crumbly. Bake 15 minutes.

While the crust is baking, make the filling. In a large bowl, beat the cream cheese until fluffy. Beat in the sour cream and then the eggs one at a time. Beat in the granulated sugar, vanilla, and lemon zest.

continued

Lemon Blueberry Cheesecake With
Shortbread Cookie Crust *(continued)*

When the crust is removed from the oven, transfer the filling to the crust, smooth down with a rubber spatula, then use the handle of a fork or spoon to swirl the blueberry jam through the filling.

Bake 1 hour, until gently set (the filling will still be a bit jiggly) and the sides are start-ing to brown lightly. Let cool completely, then cover with plastic wrap and transfer to the refrigerator. Refrigerate at least 3 hours before serving.

Serves 12

Jewish Apple Cake

This isn't an innovative or groundbreaking dessert, but I really wanted to include it because it's one of my favorite things in the world to eat. In fact, I can literally eat it all day, or any time of day. If I have it lying around the house, I'll have a slice for breakfast, a slice with some tea or coffee in the afternoon, and a slice with vanilla ice cream for dessert. If you're going to make this for dessert, then I definitely recommend the vanilla ice cream part.

For the Apples

1½ pounds Golden Delicious apples, peeled, cored, and sliced into ¼-inch slices
Juice of 1 lemon
¼ cup sugar
1 teaspoon ground cinnamon

For the Batter

4 large eggs
1½ cups vegetable oil
1 stick unsalted butter, melted
2 cups sugar
1 tablespoon pure vanilla extract
½ cup warm water
2½ cups all-purpose flour
½ teaspoon salt
1 tablespoon baking powder

Special equipment: a Bundt pan

Preheat the oven to 350°F.

Mix the apples with the lemon juice, sugar, and cinnamon in a mixing bowl and let stand while you make the batter.

Light whisk the eggs in a large mixing bowl. Add the oil, melted butter, sugar, vanilla, and water and whisk until smooth. In a separate mixing bowl, combine the flour, salt, and baking powder. Use a whisk to mix the dry ingredients together.

Gradually stir the flour mixture into the wet mixture and stir just until incorporated. Do not overmix.

Grease and lightly flour a Bundt pan. Pour one quarter of the batter into the pan, then arrange a third of the apples around the top of the batter. Make 2 more layers of apples, smoothing the batter over them after each addition. Top off with the last quarter of the batter and smooth.

Bake about 70 minutes, until risen, the top is nicely browned, and a sharp knife inserted in the middle of the cake comes out dry.

Serves 12–15

My Best Chocolate Cake Ever

What else can I say? This is tops.

For the Cake

3 eggs

1 cup full-fat (whole milk) yogurt

1 stick unsalted butter, melted

1 teaspoon pure vanilla extract

1½ cups sugar

1¼ cups all-purpose flour

¾ cup unsweetened cocoa

1½ teaspoons baking powder

1 teaspoon baking soda

Pinch salt

1 cup hot water

For the Ganache

1 cup heavy cream

12 ounces semisweet chocolate, chopped

Preheat the oven to 350°F.

In a large bowl, beat the eggs and yogurt together. Beat in the melted butter and vanilla. Gradually beat in the sugar until fully incorporated.

In a separate mixing bowl, whisk together the flour, cocoa, baking powder, baking soda, and salt until homogeneous.

Mix the dry ingredients into the wet in two steps, alternating with the hot water.

Divide the batter between two greased and floured 8- or 9-inch square or round cake pans. Bake 25 minutes, until set. Allow to cool fully.

Make the ganache: Bring the cream to a boil in a saucepan and remove from the heat. Add the chocolate pieces and whisk until dissolved into the cream and the mixture is creamy and thick. Allow to cool.

Remove one of the cake layers from its pan and place on a large serving plate. Pour half the ganache into the middle of the cake and use a spatula to spread the ganache out, allowing some ganache to fall down the sides of the cake.

Remove the other layer from its pan and place it on top of the first layer. Pour the remaining ganache on top to create a smooth, even coating. Place in the refrigerator for at least 1 hour so the ganache sets fully.

Serves 12–15

To get a neat fit between the two cake layers, cut the very top off the bottom layer with a long, serrated knife.

One Dough, Three Cookies

This is a great way to get variety without much extra effort. It's also a great way to get some really tasty cookies. Each recipe makes about 12 cookies.

Basic Dough

2 cups all-purpose flour

1 teaspoon baking soda

½ teaspoon salt

Pinch of ground cloves

2 sticks unsalted butter, softened

1 cup light brown sugar

1 cup granulated sugar

2 large eggs

1 teaspoon pure vanilla extract

Coarse "raw" sugar, for sugar cookies only

Preheat oven to 375°F.

Whisk together the flour, baking soda, salt, and cloves in a small bowl. Beat the butter and sugar in a large bowl with an electric mixer at medium-high speed until pale and fluffy, about 3 minutes. Beat in the eggs one at a time, and vanilla. Reduce the speed to low, then add the flour mixture and mix until just combined.

Form the dough into a 12-inch log (2 inches in diameter) on a sheet of plastic wrap and roll up in the plastic wrap. Chill the dough in the refrigerator for 1 hour.

Cut ½-inch-thick slices from the log with a sharp knife and arrange on two large un-greased baking sheets about 1 inch apart.

For basic sugar cookies, sprinkle gener-ously with coarse sugar and bake for 15 minutes, or until lightly browned and slightly puffed.

Cool on the baking sheets for 3 minutes, then transfer with a metal spatula to racks to cool completely.

Chocolate and Walnut Cookies

6 tablespoons cocoa powder
½ cup chopped walnuts

Make the basic dough according to the recipe above, but add the cocoa powder to the flour mixture and fold in the nuts just after mixing the batter. Bake for 15 minutes, then cool on the baking sheets for 3 minutes before transferring to racks to cool completely.

Almond-Orange Cookies

½ orange, zested
½ cup sliced almonds, finely chopped in a blender to a coarse flour consistency
24 teaspoons chunky marmalade
½ cup sliced almonds, for topping

Make the basic dough according to the recipe above, but add both the orange zest and chopped almonds when you add the flour mixture.

When the cookies are formed, make a slight depression in the middle and fill each with about 1 teaspoon marmalade. Top each with a good pinch of sliced almonds. Bake for 20 minutes, then cool on the baking sheets for 3 minutes before transferring to racks to cool completely.

Baked Apples With Brown Sugar and Tricky Custard Sauce

Here's a simple, cheap, and fast option for dessert. My dad used to make this for us during the week when we needed a quick fix. I never complained. I've added a rich vanilla cream sauce that's based on a tricky secret weapon. It's a wonder.

2 Golden Delicious apples
2 to 3 tablespoons unsalted butter
4 tablespoons light brown sugar
Ground cinnamon, for sprinkling
Creamy Custard Sauce (recipe follows)

Preheat the oven to 350°F.

Wash and dry the apples. Cut the apples in half and remove the core, but leave any stems intact. Place the apples in a baking dish. Divide the butter among each core cavity. Top each apple half with a tablespoon of sugar and a dash of cinnamon.

Bake the apples until the flesh is tender and they're bubbly and perfect looking, about 30 minutes. Serve with Creamy Custard Sauce.

Tricky Custard Sauce

½ pint light vanilla ice cream, melted
2 egg yolks

Heat the melted ice cream in a small saucepan over low heat until hot. Meanwhile, put the yolks in a mixing bowl and whisk until smooth. While whisking, slowly drizzle about 1 or 2 tablespoons hot melted ice cream into the yolks until blended.

While whisking constantly, slowly add the rest of the hot liquid to the yolk mixture. Pour the mixture back into the saucepan, return to low heat, and cook 4 to 5 minutes longer, stirring all the while, until the mixture has thickened but is still creamy.

Serves 4

Peach Corn Bread Trifle

This is a very straightforward, classic trifle with corn bread as the unclassic twist.
I came up with this recipe when I was cooking a barbecue down in Tennessee.
I was inspired by being down South and by the beautiful, fragrant peaches
that I found in the market. The quality of this dessert does depend on how good
your peaches are, so it's best (and cheapest) to make this when peaches are in
season. However, you can sometimes find really good peaches coming up from
South America in the off-season. Fresh peaches in winter are indeed a true luxury!

2 pounds very ripe peaches

2 cups heavy cream

¼ cup superfine sugar

½ teaspoon pure vanilla extract

1 pound corn bread, either store-bought or
    homemade

Remove the skins of the peaches by dropping them in a pot of simmering water for just a minute. Remove the peaches, set aside to cool, then peel off the loosened skins. Remove the pits from the peaches and finely chop the flesh. Put the chopped peaches in a bowl.

Pour the cream into a large mixing bowl. Add the sugar and vanilla and whip into soft peaks.

Cut the corn bread into thin slices. Layer the bottom of a clear glass trifle or other serving bowl with a third of the corn bread. Add a third of the peaches on top of the corn bread, then a third of the whipped cream on top of that. Repeat the layers two more times and crumble the final layer of corn bread on top.

Refrigerate and serve cold.

Serves 12–15

Pecan-Dusted Puff Pastry Caramelized Apple Napoleons

Here's an impressive dessert that I could serve at my fanciest gigs. Between the crispy pastry dough, the cream, apples, and toasted nuts, this dessert has it all.

For the Puff Pastry

1/2 cup pecans
1 tablespoon granulated sugar
1 tablespoon dark brown sugar
1/2 teaspoon ground cinnamon
1 sheet store-bought puff pastry, such as
    Pillsbury, thawed

For the Apples

1 1/2 pounds sweet firm apples (such as Gala,
    Fuji, or Golden Delicious), cut into 1/4-inch
    slices
1/2 stick unsalted butter, melted
2 tablespoons granulated sugar
2 tablespoons dark brown sugar

For the Whipped Cream

1 1/2 cups heavy cream
2 tablespoons superfine sugar
1 1/2 teaspoons pure vanilla extract

Preheat the oven to 400°F.

Chop the pecans to the consistency of rough crumbs. Toss with the sugars and cinnamon in a small bowl. Spread the mixture out onto a baking sheet and cook in the oven 7 to 10 minutes, until darkened and lightly caramelized. Set aside to cool.

Roll out the puff pastry on a floured surface to 1/16-inch thickness. Cut the puff pastry sheet into 12 squares, approximately 3 × 3 inches. Lay out on a baking sheet and bake 15 minutes, until puffed and golden brown. Remove from the oven and set aside to cool.

Toss together the apples, melted butter, and sugars in a 13 × 9-inch baking dish. Bake the apples 30 minutes, stirring every 5 minutes for even browning, until soft and a rich golden brown.

Whip the cream, granulated sugar, and vanilla in a mixing bowl until it forms soft peaks.

Place a puff pastry square in the center of a serving bowl or plate. Sprinkle with pecans, then top with a generous dollop of whipped cream, a few apples, and a good pinch of pecan pieces. Then stack another pastry square on top and finish with a second spoonful of whipped cream, more apples, and a dash of pecans. Repeat this process until all the ingredients are used up.

Serves 6

Sweet Crepes

Making crepes is actually a lot of fun when you're having a casual get-together and your friends can keep you company as you turn them out. If you've never had the experience, it's something you definitely should try. I "studied" the technique of making them when I was living in Paris for a summer, where I frequented the local crepe stand a little too often. There are no rules when it comes to toppings, so I've just given you a list of some of my favorites. You can take it from there.

For the Crepes

¾ cup all-purpose flour

1 teaspoon salt

1 cup milk, preferably whole

2 eggs, lightly beaten

2 tablespoons sugar

1 tablespoon butter, melted, plus more for cooking the crepes

½ teaspoon pure vanilla extract

Serving Suggestions

All kinds of jams

Butter

Honey

Sugar

Nutella

Peanut butter

Sliced bananas

Put the flour and salt in a large mixing bowl. Gradually whisk in the milk. Whisk in the eggs, then the sugar, melted butter, and vanilla. Cover and let rest in the refrigerator for about 1 hour.

Heat an 8-inch nonstick skillet over medium-high heat. Melt a small pat of butter in the pan and swirl around so that it lightly coats the surface.

Add ⅓ cup of the batter, moving your wrist in a circular pattern to coat the pan with a thin, even layer of batter. Cook for about 1 minute, or until the first side browns lightly, then flip and cook 1 minute longer. Remove to a plate and repeat with the remaining batter.

Fill with topping of choice—anything sweet that you enjoy from your pantry.

Makes about 8 crepes

Banana Mash Cake
With Coconut-Sour Cream Icing

For the Cake

2 cups granulated sugar

2 sticks unsalted butter, melted

4 eggs

2 teaspoons pure vanilla extract

$^2/_3$ cup sour cream

2 pounds very ripe bananas, mashed

3 cups all-purpose flour

2 teaspoons salt

2 teaspoons baking soda

For the Icing

$^1/_2$ stick unsalted butter, melted

$^1/_2$ cup sour cream

1 pound confectioners' sugar

$^1/_4$ pound shredded coconut, plus a couple
   tablespoons more for garnish

Preheat the oven to 350°F.

Whisk together the granulated sugar, melted butter, eggs, vanilla, and sour cream in a large mixing bowl until smooth and thoroughly incorporated. In a separate bowl, whisk together the dry ingredients. Gradually combine the dry ingredients into the wet. Pour the batter into a greased 10-inch Bundt pan.

Make the icing: Whisk together all the ingredients in a mixing bowl until smooth and thick. Let cool before using.

Bake about 70 minutes, until set and golden brown on top. Let cool before removing from the pans. Cut each cake in half horizontally. Use one of the halves as the base for the layer cake. Top with a quarter of the icing, then top with another cake half. Repeat until all layers are used. Finish by icing the top and scattering the remaining coconut over the top of the cake. Let the icing set before serving.

Beet Mash Chocolate Cake With Beet Frosting

For the Cake

1 pound beets
2 sticks unsalted butter, melted
½ cup vegetable oil
2½ cups granulated sugar
3 eggs
½ cup warm water
1½ cups all-purpose flour
¾ cup unsweetened cocoa
2 teaspoons baking powder
½ teaspoon salt

For the Icing

2 sticks unsalted butter
1 small beet, finely mashed
1 pound confectioners' sugar

Cook the beets in a pot of boiling water until fork-tender, about 1 hour. Rinse under cold water, trim, and peel. Mash finely with a potato masher.

Preheat the oven to 325°F.

In a large mixing bowl, whisk together the melted butter, granulated sugar, eggs, and water.

In a separate bowl, whisk together the dry ingredients until thoroughly combined. Gradually mix the dry ingredients into the wet. Fold in the beets and mix well.

Pour the batter into a greased 10-inch Bundt pan. Bake about 70 minutes, until set but moist. Let cool, then turn out onto a large serving plate.

Make the icing: Melt 1 stick of butter in a saucepan together with the mashed beet. Simmer on very low heat for 5 minutes. Meanwhile, cream the second stick of butter with a mixer in a bowl. Mix in the melted butter and beet mixture until fully incorporated. Gradually beat in the confectioners' sugar.

Ice the cake with a thick layer of icing.

Each cake serves 12–15

Cranberry-Almond Chocolate Bars
With Tangerine Zest

This is a no-fuss chocolate treat. It's pretty much pure chocolate with some extras, so a little goes a long way. I like to have a piece with coffee at the end of a meal. The citrus and cranberries add a cleansing quality to the bars.

½ cup slivered almonds
3 cups bittersweet or semisweet chocolate
    morsels
½ cup dried cranberries
Zest of ½ tangerine

Preheat the oven to 400°F.

Line a 13 × 9-inch baking pan with aluminum foil.

Lay out the almond slivers on a baking sheet. Bake until light brown, shaking the baking pan occasionally to mix them, about 10 to 15 minutes.

Melt the chocolate morsels in a double boiler over low heat. Mix in the cranberries, almond slivers, and tangerine zest.

Pour into the prepared pan. Smooth the chocolate mixture out into an even layer. Cool to room temperature, then refrigerate until hard, at least 1 hour. Use a knife to break up the chocolate into jagged, varied-size bars.

Two Mini Semifreddo Cupcakes

Semifreddos are a foolproof way to get the experience and taste of ice cream without fancy equipment. Here are two unique flavors that are a fun twist on common ice cream flavors.

Lemon Poppy Seed Sour Cream

4 egg yolks
½ cup sugar
1 teaspoon pure vanilla extract
Juice and grated zest of ½ lemon
2 tablespoons poppy seeds
¼ cup sour cream
1 cup heavy (whipping) cream

Paper muffin cups

Whip the cream until it forms soft peaks.

Bring a couple inches of water to a boil in a large pot. Whisk together the egg yolks, sugar, vanilla, and lemon juice in a heatproof bowl. Place over the pot of boiling water. Whisk constantly until the mixture thickens and becomes a pale yellow. Remove from the heat.

Mix in the poppy seeds and the sour cream.

Fold the whipped cream into the lemon-egg mixture and pour into paper cup–lined cupcake tins. Freeze at least 2 hours.

Peel away the paper cup liners, place on a serving plate, and garnish with the lemon zest.

Chocolate Cardamom

1 cup heavy cream
4 egg yolks
⅓ cup sugar
1 teaspoon pure vanilla extract
¼ teaspoon ground cardamom
3 tablespoons unsweetened cocoa
Orange zest

Paper muffin cups

Whip the heavy cream in a bowl until it forms soft peaks.

Bring a couple of inches of water to a boil in a large pot.

Whisk together the egg yolks, sugar, vanilla, and cardamom in a heatproof bowl. Place over a pot of boiling water. Whisk constantly until the mixture thickens and becomes pale yellow. Whisk in the cocoa, whisk a minute or two longer, then remove from the heat.

Fold the whipped cream into the chocolate-egg mixture and pour into paper cup–lined cupcake tins. Freeze at least 2 hours.

Peel away the paper cup liners, place on a serving plate, and garnish with orange zest.

Each recipe makes about
8 mini semifreddos

Acknowledgments

Thank you:

Will Schwalbe, Ellen Archer, and Bob Miller for believing in me and my work and making beautiful books. Will Schwalbe and Leslie Wells for your support and editing throughout the process. Miriam Wenger for holding together all the loose ends, and everyone else at Hyperion for doing such great work.

Lisa Queen for guiding and championing my way.

Wes Martin, for spending so much time with me in the beginning, critical stages of the book, developing concepts and recipes, and generally keeping me happy with your company.

George Whiteside, an incredible photographer and a good friend. Thank you for making such beautiful photos yet again. Thanks also to the Toronto photo crew, Anthea and Katya, for making those long days smooth and fun. And Adele Hagan for helping make the food look its best.

Bob Tuschman, Brooke Johnson, Doug Parker, Lia Wiedemann, Christiana Reinhardt, Karlyn Ferrari, Susan Stockton, Rob Bleifer, Jill Novak, and all the rest of my friends and colleagues at Food Network who give me the chance to do what I love in front of a camera and help me to do it better.

Sian Edwards, for believing in me from the very beginning, being my ally, and for making some of the best food television out there! Also, of course, Sarah Teale, Jimmy Choi, Laurie Buck, Carly Jacobs,

Kevin Liesek, Rob Krisch, Croi McNamara, Jay Mitchell, Herb Forsberg, Alan Jacobsen, Mike Larini, Billy Kent, Betsy Hart, and everybody else from Teale Edwards productions for all the hard work it takes to make my cooing come to life.

Lisa Shotland for being on the frontlines for me so that I can do the fun stuff!

And of course to all my wonderful family and friends.

Index

205